# GROWING UP ALASKA

Memories of a Town, a Time,
a Place, and a People Planted in
a Little Pocket of Wonderful

## by Niki Breeser Tschirgi

First published by Dog Ear Publishing
4011 Vincennes Rd
Indianapolis, IN 46268
www.dogearpublishing.net

ISBN: 978-1-4575-3771-4

This book is printed on acid-free paper.

Printed in the United States of America

This book is dedicated to my dad, Steve Breeser. He dreamed of Alaska. . . . Then he lived his dream and took us along with him. Thank you, Dad. Without you, there would be no *Growing up Alaska*.

In loving memory

July 14, 1949–April 4, 1996

Me and my dad outside of our home in Tok at the Bureau of Land Management (BLM) pump station.

# Acknowledgments

Special thanks to my mom, Marsha Breeser. Her support, love, and courage over the years have been crucial in the shaping of me. She, along with my dad, instilled in me a spirit of adventure that cannot be curbed, as well as a solid faith in God, Who cannot be moved. Because she was willing to follow "her man" into the wilds of Alaska, I am who I am today. Wild and free, that is me. Maybe, just maybe, that is you too.

Mom, Cid, and me. I am so grateful my mom had her camera handy during my growing up years. Most of the pictures in this book were taken by her.

Thank you to my husband, Matt, for always believing in my dream to publish and to my children, who have cheered me on along the way. They may roll their eyes as I tell them another Alaska story, but that's okay. I had a great childhood, and I will tell their children and their children's children. I will tell them about the good old days. The good old days in Tok.

Thank you to the people of Tok. To my teachers, coaches, neighbors, business owners, classmates, and friends, and especially to my brother Cid. *You* are this book. The community of Tok is why I still treasure my childhood today. Yes, the great frontier was part of it and is still in my heart, but the people, you, are what take up the most room. Thank you.

Thank you to Paul Kelley, Beth Jacobs, and Ellen Splitt for added information and pictures, and to Auntie Barb Breeser for helping with the editing process.

Thank you to *all* of you who supported me during my crowd fund to publish this book. Your enthusiasm, monetary support, encouragement, and proud display of decals and hoodies has touched me deeply. I could not have done this without you. When I started to question the sanity of what I was doing, I would get a message from someone encouraging me. I needed every single one of your kind words. I needed every single ounce of your support. Thank you.

# Contents

# Foreword

## By Marsha Breeser

G*rowing up Alaska* contains engaging and endearing glimpses into the life of Niki Breeser Tschirgi. Niki resided in Tok, Alaska, from March 1982 through July 1992. For her, Tok will always be home. I am reminded of an event shortly after her arrival in Tok at the ripe old age of six. Her first-grade class performed a song during a school concert. There was Niki, singing her heart out like she had been there forever! She may have even been waving the state flag. I think she knew she was home!

It was always her dad's dream to live in Alaska. We had tried to make it our home in the summer of 1971, despite warnings at the borders that there were no jobs in Alaska, which proved correct, at least for us. Nevertheless, in 1982, as a family, we made our way across Montana and Washington, boarded the *Columbia* (the Alaska state ferry), and headed north. We could not help but notice various students onboard getting on or off the ferry at points along the way. We found out that travel by ferry was the order of the day if students were to compete in school-sponsored events. Soon, extended travel would be a part of Niki's life, too: jets, ferries, and many tours by school bus, usually with windows frosted over and probably frozen shut!

Niki reminiscences about growing up in Alaska; I join her in this reminiscence. Her first daily adventure was trudging through the snow, flashlight in hand, to catch the school bus on winter mornings. Later, as a family, we would be charged by a moose while out canoeing. As I read these stories, however, I wondered, *Whatever was I thinking at times in regard to her safety and survival?* On my part, some ignorance was probably bliss, and in fairness to myself, I was usually the one to sound the alarm if I thought something was amiss! Was I ever secretly glad when certain opportunities fell through (such as a helicopter ride as a class field trip, or cancelled road trips that would have taken her far beyond my reach in the extreme cold)? Yes!

Life within a small community framed her days, and life in a state unique by its own standards added an extra dimension of adventure to her life. Whether you live in Alaska, have lived there (no matter how long), have visited, or dream of exploring this great state, settle back and enjoy adventures, antics, and interesting characters.

As an adult, Niki has captured a wistful glance back at the simple yet captivating details of a life lived *Growing up Alaska.*

Here's to reminiscing the fine points of her childhood. . . . Here's to *Growing up Alaska.*

Marsha Breeser at Moon Lake.

# Introduction: A Note from Niki

Cid, me, and my dad gold panning.

There is just something about Alaska. No matter where you go, after you have lived in Alaska, you still feel connected. Maybe a truck drives by with the Alaska license plate or Alaska bumper sticker and you wonder out loud if you know the driver. You might even imagine yourself following them, getting out of your car, and asking them. Perhaps you cry sweet tears of homecoming as you fly into Anchorage after a many-year absence. Once an Alaskan, always an Alaskan.

This book is for those of you who grew up there but left and fondly remember your crazy, freezing, and totally awesome childhood. It's also for those who have visited and gotten a taste. It's for those who have thought about going or dreamed about going, and it's for those who have never considered the trip. Finally, this book is for those of you who stayed. It's for those of you there in the right-here and the right-now, making new memories of *Growing up Alaska*.

We who have moved on may be just a little bit jealous. Just a little . . .

# Arriving Alaska

# A Father's Dream

The Port of Seattle. The Columbia ferry docked, 1982.

O ur move up to Alaska included a three-day ferry ride on the *Columbia*. We drove from far northeastern Montana to the coast of Washington. That was the most normal part of our trip. My dad drove the truck and my mom the little Nissan Datsun 210. Tucked firmly in the trunk of her little car were one hundred pounds of wheat. A friend on the prairie had given my mom an electric grain mill and the wheat because she was moving to Alaska. That was her way of saying thank you and of gifting my mom for the years of friendship. It was a practical gift, to be sure. My mom was able to grind wheat and feed us bread for a year or longer because of that friend's provision, and she still has that wheat grinder today. My mom also had squirreled away between the two vehicles her canned tomatoes, pickle relish, and pounds and pounds of frozen venison. Everything was iced and packed for our long journey north.

Besides the food provisions split between the two vehicles, there was also me; my brother; our dog, Annie; and some clothes. The US Fish and Wildlife Service was moving all of our furniture, but it wouldn't arrive until about a week after we got to

Tok, so we had some essentials for the trip. We stayed one night in Montana and then a night in Moses Lake, Washington, before we arrived in Seattle to spend one more night before boarding the ferry. After settling in at the hotel, we found out that we could rent fishing poles and fish out of the window. What was this place, on the ocean? I had left the prairie for something very different from what I had known. Gone were the waving fields of prairie grass and wheat. In their place were giant trees, mountains, rivers, lakes, and an ocean that sprawled as far as the eye could see. I had never seen the ocean before, and I wasn't even close to being in Alaska yet.

The next day, we boarded the ferry, and it was quite late at night (maybe even close to midnight) when we finally launched out into the gray, freezing Pacific. People were standing at the back of the boat, with the deck fairly bursting. All of a sudden, the hum of excited chatter was drowned out by the ferry engines. As we collectively turned our eyes to the departing shore, the chatter ceased and only the quiet roar of the engine and the water splashing about the boat could be heard. The mood was somber as the lights of Seattle grew smaller and smaller, the Space Needle becoming a blip in the distance among the tall office buildings. What were the other passengers thinking at that moment? Were they like us, a family on the move to a new life? Were they running away from something, or to something or someone? No matter what we were thinking, the land that we had known faded away into blackness as the boat plowed on through the choppy ocean water.

By the time we had gotten on the boat and began our journey, it was well past time to sleep. We had a cabin, but I vividly remember people sleeping on the deck with their sleeping bags and blankets, trying to keep warm on the deck chairs. They were wild-looking wilderness people, very much the wandering sort or the adventure-seeking sort. The ferry had a cafeteria that sold snack food and a sit-down dining room, along with several observation decks. We noticed the salt and pepper shakers were weighted down so they wouldn't slide off the tables, a look into what we could expect on our ocean journey.

Over the course of the three-day ferry ride, there were times when open ocean was to the west of us and land to the east, causing great swells to rock our boat (hence the weighted salt and pepper shakers). My dad and brother, Cid, were unaffected by the heaving and swaying motion. They would stand on the observation deck until they were the last ones there. My mom and I, however, did not fare quite as well and huddled in our berth, attempting to keep our lunches down. Earlier, when we had taken off out of Seattle, the captain had come on the speaker and announced that the ship's store didn't have any Dramamine and wouldn't be getting any until a much later date. That would have been good information to know *before* we had launched, as we were already cutting through the waves with our compass pointed north.

Cid and me onboard the Columbia ferry.

Our first major stop was Ketchikan, Alaska. During the ride, the crew would announce different times for people to go down to the cargo hold, where all of our vehicles were, to tend to our pets, which were kenneled in the cars and trucks. At the front of the boat by the vehicles was an area for the dogs to poop. No dog would poop there. Annie, our dog, refused. We would take her out and walk her around, but to no avail. That dog (along with countless others) would not eat, poop, or pee on that boat. When we arrived in Ketchikan, however, we got off the boat with Annie and she was more than happy to do her business. I'm sure when the ferry first started carrying passengers, the people of Ketchikan weren't planning on the boatloads of dogs doing their duty on the pristine shoreline.

On the final day of our trip, the ferry landed in Haines, Alaska. I distinctly remember the plethora of bald eagles. They were everywhere. We couldn't get in to Haines right away because no one was at the border station yet, so we had to all line up in our vehicles and wait to get off the boat.

After we unloaded from the ferry, we were still about twelve hours from Tok, so on our way to our new home, we stopped for the night and stayed at the White River Lodge in the Yukon Territory. My mom referred to it as a resort. I begged to differ.

It was −38° when we pulled up to the "resort." All of the meat that my dad had packed to take up to our new home had slightly thawed on the ferry but was now refrozen solid in the shockingly subzero temperatures of Canada.

We were the final travelers of the day to secure hotel rooms, but we weren't the final travelers to arrive that night. My dad paid for the last two rooms, with my dad and mom in one room and my brother and I in another. Good thing we weren't abducted. Housing your six and nine-year-olds in a separate room in a foreign country would not be done by most Americans today. The rooms were tiny. White River Lodge reminded my parents somewhat of mobile trailers attached together end to end. There was a communal bathroom for us four in the two rooms to share with a metal shower. At least it was clean, but at −38°, a metal shower wasn't exactly an ideal bathing situation, nor was the fact that we had to share it.

After settling into our rooms (which included my dad carrying in four boxes of canned tomatoes (forty-eight quarts) so they wouldn't freeze overnight), we returned to the dining area to have dinner. When we had walked into the lodge, our eyes had alighted on a few tables making up the dining room, and a small store. Through a door, we caught a glimpse of the owner's living room. People kept on showing up looking for lodging, and I know my mom couldn't help but wonder what we would have done if we had happened upon the lodge even a few minutes later.

White River Lodge, Yukon Territory. My dad is heading toward the white door, and I am standing at the back of our truck by the coolers full of venison. I imagine my dad was hauling out all of my mom's canned tomatoes for our final leg of the trip to Tok.

Sitting down in the dining room, my dad perused the menu. Everything he asked for, they were out of. After four tries, my dad gently set down his menu and with a twinkle in his eyes said, "Well, what *do* you have?" They had a few shrimp left, so that is what he had. This was our first taste of life way up north…and it wouldn't be our last.

We arrived at the Alaska–Canada border the next day. My mom and dad flashed their driver's licenses, and we were in. We pulled over in the freezing sunshine for a picture. The old rickety sign that said, "Welcome to Alaska," had a spray-painted message on the bottom for us. It said, "Leave while you still can." My mom's over-all thought of our family's trip north compared to her first trip up with just my dad on their honeymoon was that this time, it was a luxury. The last time, on their honeymoon, they had lived in a tent and couldn't find work. We, on the other hand, had come up on a ferry, had been able to eat in a cafeteria and dining room on the boat, and, instead of sleeping in a tent, had slept in a lodge . . . and to top it off, my dad had a job. I guess it truly is all about perspective.

My mom will never forget the drive from the border to Tok. She was driving the little Datsun with my brother in the backseat. She was going around a curve and ended up doing some wild donuts. Cid, my brother, calmly and curiously asked

Alaska-Canada border, "Leave while you still can."

her, "Why are you doing donuts, Mom?" She thought, *I didn't intend to do that donut,* but kept that information to herself.

There had been a freak ice storm, and the roads were glare ice, so my mom drove the last thirty miles wondering where the salt was for the roads. What she didn't know was that salt doesn't work at that cold of a temperature. It would be years before sand was introduced to help keep the roads safer.

Literally sliding into Tok and grateful for the hundred pounds of wheat in the trunk of the car, my mom wondered aloud, "Where is it?" There wasn't much to look at. It was quite desolate on that cold, March day. We stopped in at my dad's new Fish and Wildlife office, located right next door to Frontier Foods grocery store. My mom recalls the wood floor creaking as we took in our little store, surveying what was to be our new life. That first week, we stayed at the Golden Bear Motel, waiting for our furniture to arrive. During that time, my parents painted the apartment, getting our new place ready for the arrival of our goods. During that time, we began to settle. During that time, I started growing up Alaska.

# Living the Dream

Phyllis and Walt Breeser, my dad's parents, outside the original
Fish and Wildlife Service office in Tok.

My earliest memories of the US Fish and Wildlife Service are in Montana. We lived right on the refuge on the shores of Medicine Lake situated near a tiny town with the same name in the northeastern corner of the state. My brother and I would go out in the early morning with our dad to help him band ducks. I can see the shore even all these years later. My dad and other staff of the refuge would shoot a net out over the birds, and after the birds were caught, my brother and I would "help" put the metal band around their leg and let them go. I knew from a very young age that my dad was built for the outdoors and the outdoors was where he would stay. As a young boy in Iowa, he had gone fishing before school and hunting for squirrels after. He was born for the outdoor life. It was evident that on the land and among the wildlife was where he belonged and where he needed to be.

It was the US Fish and Wildlife Service that ultimately led to our trek up to Alaska. I'm not sure how long it was in my dad's heart to live in the Great Land, but I know it dated back to at least the early seventies. He had attempted to get a job up there while newly married to my mom. As she recalls, they drove up with all the money they had in their pockets, and if the money ran out before the job transpired, well, then back down to the Midwest they would go, but my dad had to try. It did look pretty hopeless when they got to the Alaskan border and there were signs posted to turn around now because there were no jobs. But when a man has a dream in his heart, a tent in his car, and money in his pocket, he has to at least try, so they did. They drove around Alaska looking for work and living in a tent, and yes, you guessed it, their money ran down to enough for a return trip, so back south to the States they went.

From there, Dad worked on the Upper Mississippi and then in Montana, always keeping Alaska in his sights. It would be nearly ten years after his honeymoon trip when the job at the Tetlin National Wildlife Refuge came across his path and the door to Alaska would fly wide open.

I wouldn't have grown up in Alaska if it hadn't been for my dad. His love for the land and his dream to work in Alaska are what gave me and my brother the beloved childhood we had. I always knew that my dad was exactly where he needed to be, wherever his job might take him. Whether it was on the banks of the Upper Mississippi River, the shores of Medicine Lake, the acres upon acres of land he flew to on the Tetlin National Wildlife Refuge, or the shallow waters of Lake Umbagog in New Hampshire, he was always at home educating the people and conserving the land that he so loved.

# Home Sweet Home

My dad teaching the kids of Tok and the surrounding areas about wildlife.

After our move to the little town of Tok, our first housing assignment was at the Bureau of Land Management (BLM) pump station. They were old apartments dating back to WWII and designed for the living conditions in the South Pacific. Someone had the bright idea to build them in Alaska. I'm sure the government loved the heating bill those places ran up. My mom probably cried in the cold corner, but my dad . . . my dad was so happy.

Situated seven miles outside of town, my brother and I and other kids living out there would walk up the long road to the highway for the school bus to pick us up to take us in to Tok. Busing to school wasn't new to us, since we'd lived outside of town on the refuge in Montana. The only difference was how much colder it was now as we walked to the bus stop.

Things changed for us kids, though, regarding my dad and his job. In Montana, we'd lived right on the refuge, often traveling with our dad and learning the birds, fish, and vegetation of the land. This new job had my dad flying to the refuge, so

---

Me, standing on the hill behind the pump station.
Our apartments were right behind me.

our knowledge of this new place was greatly reduced, given the vastness of the refuge and the difficulty of actually setting foot on it. But oh, how he loved it.

Usually, the people who work for Fish and Wildlife move quite a bit, but God had his hand on this journey and kept us settled in Tok for over ten years. Maybe it would have been longer, but my dad had another dream that stretched beyond Alaska, and that was to help start a brand-new wildlife refuge, so in the summer of 1992, we would pack up our home, our vehicles, and all of the people in our hearts and drive to New Hampshire for my dad to live what would be the final part of his dream. Before his passing in 1996, he was able to help secure the land and see his dream fulfilled in the creation of Lake Umbagog National Wildlife Refuge. He was able to preside over the refuge dedication, but not over the new office complex that was dedicated in his memory. On the day of the refuge dedication, a beam of sunlight would shine on my dad's empty chair, a sign from heaven above: He had completed his dream. He had completed his journey. But most importantly, he had lived it and lived it well.

Mom, Matt, Me, Tammy, and Cid at the refuge dedication.
We are standing by the plaque honoring my dad.

# Childhood

# Wild and Free

Cid, me, and our mom, Marsha.

Wild and free, that was me. You could see it in my hair, in my eyes, and in my unmatched clothing. Now, granted, the hair was a little billowy and wild because yes, it was the early eighties, but more importantly, it was Tok. Who gets their hair cut in Tok? At that time, nobody, because there was nobody around to do it. My mom told me later in life after I made loving comments about our hippy look that we were hippy by default. I just knew I loved it—jeans, t-shirts, old hoodies, worn-out shoes, and flannel.

I can remember digging through my old dresser where we first lived (at the pump station) when I was around eight years old for an outfit. I couldn't believe my luck! I had just been told I could pick out what to wear. My mom must have reached a point where she was able to just let go and let us dress ourselves for better or for worse. I think Alaska does that to you, helps you let go. I chose a white shirt with red sleeves, with a pair of giant cherries on it (outlined in silver iron-on sparkles) and a pair of purple shorts. Then I randomly grabbed a colorful pair of socks. I thought, *Who cares about the socks? They don't matter anyway, because they are just on my feet!* I took one look at myself after I was all clad in red cherries, purple shorts, and mismatched socks, and thought, *Beautiful.*

I went about my day like that, with my dirty-blonde overgrown hair getting constantly shoved out of my eyes by my little hands so I could see and live my wild and adventurous life. I had on my sturdy burgundy—yes, burgundy—kangaroo sneakers and nothing-matching clothing, and that was just fine by me, to be wild and free. To me, it was just a matter of clothing myself to get on with the day. The good part of the day. The playing part of the day. There was no second look in the mirror to see if my makeup was on just right or my hair was smoothed just so. I didn't do three turns in the mirror to catch every angle and then tear off my outfit in disgust and toss it aside while I rummaged for a new one. Shoot, I didn't even run a comb through my hair! I was clothed! I was ready! I was as unspoiled as the land that surrounded me, and after I thumped down the stairs in my gloriously unmatched outfit, I catapulted myself out the front door so I could squint my eyes at the sky.

Racing down the gravel road to meet up with the neighbor boys to work on our fort, I kicked up the dust behind me, leaving a trail of remembrance. Later, maybe we would swing at the old playground or dig in the garden. We might even march around behind the dog kennels, picking low-bush cranberries to chew on or stomp on (whatever was our fancy that day), and plucking tea leaves to bring home to boil. We would most certainly jump on our bikes and ride recklessly around all of the apartment buildings and their adjoining sidewalks. Then we'd go off road (or off sidewalk) and pedal madly over the rough-cut roads crisscrossing the terrain. I didn't even know that I was wild and free. I just was. Looking back now, though, I know. Looking back now, I can see. I can see how wild and free one can be.

Me on my bike at the BLM pump station.

# Winter Play

Me ice skating on the man-made rink at the pump station.

There was a time as a child when all was right in the world and my stress was related to what I was going to play, who I was going to play with, and if I was even going to get to play at all. Would I go outside and climb and slide down the giant snow berms that the plows had created in front of our BLM apartments? Would I beg my brother for a chilly ride on the snow machine? Granted, it was never a good deal when we went deep into the woods and got stuck and could not get unstuck in the freshly fallen snow. That meant a long walk back to the apartments and an even longer lecture from my mom when we arrived home stiff and frozen without our beloved transportation, helmets in hand. Then we would have to wait until our dad got home to dig us out of the snow pit we had gotten ourselves stuck in. Breaking trail as kids sometimes didn't go quite as we planned.

Maybe I'd stay in and play the Atari 5200 and try to master Super Breakout, a challenge at the time that seemed nearly impossible. I could always snuggle up and read

Laura Ingalls Wilder for the fifth time or knock on the door of my neighbor down the block to play with their new Ewok village from the ever-so-exciting *Return of the Jedi* movie. Yes, there were days we played inside, but most of my memories were of being cold in the snow and the brilliant yet not even close to warm sunshine of Alaska.

Every once in a while, somebody, and I don't even know who, would create an ice-skating rink for us kids who lived so far out of town. I imagine they came out with a fire truck and hose and gushed water until there was enough to skate on. There, frozen underneath the drifts of snow that had to be shoveled was a treasured floor of ice that we skated on until our toes about froze in our ever-so-thin figure skates. I knew it was time to go home when I lost all feeling in my fingers and toes and when I tried to wiggle my nose and it felt like a pickle. Then, and only then, was I ready to hang up my skates. Besides, I knew it wasn't really over. After all, tomorrow was another day for winter play.

# Kids Will Be Kids

Me and the neighbor boys playing in front of our apartments.

We kids made our own fun growing up. Like many other kids in the Lower 48, we were sent outside to erase our boredom. This was the time before super high tech home video games, Internet, cell phones, and home computers. This was the time of gathering at dusk (which is daylight during an Alaskan summer) to play kick the can. After dinner, the front doors of our apartments opened and kids of all ages scurried out to the gravel parking lot to play. Sometimes, classmates from town, like Seth Donnelly, showed up to play too. Picking someone to be "it," we would set up the old Folgers can right in the middle of the parking lot, and as the "it" person counted to ten, we would all go running, hoping to find a good hiding place. Then we would hope we wouldn't be caught, and if we got caught and put in "jail," we hoped someone would outwit the "it" person and free us by kicking the can and screaming, "Ally ally oxen free."

If kick the can wasn't on the schedule for the night, we rode our bikes from door to door. These daylight-turned-play light hours were the time when memories were

---

made. When we tired of games or bikes, we moved on to more unconventional plans, like dressing up as clowns. Who knows where I found the face paint, but I was a kid on a mission one day, and like the Pied Piper, I recruited others to join my circus. We didn't march in a parade or go to a party, but it was summer and there was time to kill for us and for our moms. Dressing up as clowns seemed as good an idea as any, and my younger neighborhood cohorts were willing guinea pigs as I worked my makeup magic. Sitting on the tiny patchy grass lawn in front of our home with barrels cut in half and raised off the ground behind us to grow our tiny gardens, in our minds, we were normal kids ready for our moms to take a picture of our handiwork. That was our normal, letting our imagination be our play. Like clown paint for no reason on a dry summer day in a little town in Alaska. We were just a bunch of kids finding something, anything, to do.

# Beloved and Not So Beloved Pets

Me, Bebop, Dad, and Mom.

W e always had some type of animal around while we were growing up, and usually more than one. I'm not talking about wild moose, caribou, and buffalo or bear, either. Annie the Springer Spaniel moved up from Montana with us. She was a sweet brown and white dog and very faithful to the end. I had hamsters and parakeets, and my dad had a fish tank full of neon tetras. Then there was my brother. My brother had a midnight-black cat named Bebop. Yes, the cat was named after a break-dance move, and yes, this was in the eighties. Believe it or not, the kids of Tok, Alaska, laid out their cardboard in the basement and attempted back spins, head spins, and various other moves they failed to master. But I digress. I was talking about a cat. You see, my dad was not a cat lover. He never was, and I would assume that if he were alive today, he would continue to be a kind and tolerating man of the animal but certainly no lover of kitties. He also never wanted a cat in the house, but that was what he got when he went off hunting for a while and left his wife and kids at home.

One day while my dad was on one such trip, my mom thought it would be fun to go see some of our neighbor's new kittens. There they were, so cute and fluffy, and in the midst of all of those kittens was a little black ball of delight. My brother immediately latched on to her, and my mom, certain of her decision, told him that if they came back later and the black kitten was still there, it was his. Now, my mother was of course thinking that there was no way that the kitten would be there after the weekend, since they were flying off the shelves like mosquito dope in summertime. What harm could there be in making a surefire promise like that to her little boy? Everyone would win (meaning my parents, not my brother); she wouldn't be the bad guy for saying no, and my dad wouldn't be mad that there was a cat in the house (let alone know it had been considered), and Cid would simply learn the lesson that life wasn't fair and his parents had tried to give him what he wanted. It wasn't like Mom had said no, so the score would be parents one, kids zero . . . the way every parent likes it to be.

Of course, you know the end of the story. Sure enough, mom took us back there, and of all those kitties, that little black ball of delight was the lone straggler, so we left with one extra passenger in the car. Kids one, parents zero . . . the way every kid likes it to be. I would have loved to have been present when my dad tromped into the house after being away on his hunting trip and heard my mom explain to him why there was a cat rubbing up against his legs, but I wasn't, and Bebop stayed. Every once in a while as the years passed, I'd catch my dad slyly petting the cat that he more than learned to tolerate.

# A Mother's Instinct

Me standing by our canoe.

I imagine that if you grew up in Alaska, you may have one or two wildlife adventures under your belt. When I was a kid we spent many a day or evening at Moon Lake, a quiet, peaceful lake shaped like a crescent moon and located fifteen miles northwest of Tok. We spent our hours wading along the shore, trying to catch the itty-bitty minnows or shrimp-looking critters. We swam out to the rafts anchored in the lake, only to return to shore with some passengers known as leeches. The tourists during the summer would get a kick out of us kids swimming in the cold water (often taking pictures), but to us kids, it was just what you did. You swam in the lake that was freezing cold, knowing you'd have to pull off leeches, maybe more than once a day. We had no local pool.

More often than not, there was a float plane tied up, maybe even two, along the shore. We'd even get to see float planes land and take off. As tourists ahh'd over the spectacle with fingers pointing and cameras clicking, we simply pulled off another leech as a float plane landed behind us. We had picnics (you could camp, but we never did). I think some people even water-skied but our family's usual mode of transportation on the lake was a simple aluminum canoe.

One afternoon, my mom, dad, and brother and I were canoeing around the lake when we happened on a mama moose and her twin babies. As we drew closer, we didn't know that she had calves with her. Moose are usually pretty docile if they are alone, but if they have their young, they will not hesitate to run you off or run you down. As we drew closer and closer, that moose got the look of death in her eyes and charged us like she just didn't care. Over a thousand pounds of mean mama moose came barreling down on our canoe. I could barely register what was happening. The enormous animal made huge waves as she pressed on to scare us off or take us out, whichever came first. I have never seen my dad, mom, and brother paddle so fast. I was the passenger in the middle, sitting cross-legged, and by the time the charging, adrenaline, paddling, and shouting were over, I was a sopping, soaking, crying mess.

My brother was quite young, and he was paddling so quickly as he sat on his knees that he was only skimming the surface of the lake, which deposited buckets and buckets of lake water on my unsuspecting head. There were tears and plenty of shaking from us kids that day, but even though I was soaked and shaking, I was safe. Safe and headed in the opposite direction of that maniac mama moose. Grateful to be out of harm's way I peaked at my mom in front of me as her paddle glided swiftly and assuredly through the water. I had a thankfulness in my heart that not only was that beast of an animal fierce and protective of her young that day, but that the curly-haired woman now sitting tranquilly in front of me was too. I learned that day about a mother's instinct, a lesson I would not soon forget.

# The Unspoiled Land and Its Rare Beauty

My dad and me off the Taylor Highway.

I often mention to my husband and my kids that because I spent the majority of my childhood in Alaska, I didn't really take the time to appreciate the beauty of the land. I suppose that is how it may be for any kid growing up: You live, laugh, love, play, and get in trouble, and the days, weeks, and years pass without you really being truly aware of your surroundings. Sometimes I think about how, literally right in my back yard, the Alaska Range towered and wild raspberries grew ripe for easy picking and eating on the giant hill behind our home at the pump station. To me at the time, however, it was simply home, the land I lived in, amidst the beauty. The land I lived life in, amidst the fireweed.

Fireweed was everywhere. It would push up through the paved bike path, blooming wildly along the highway in the ditches as we sailed past it and over it, headed out to play or work. I picked oodles of these flowers on lazy afternoons and put them in vases for my mom. I spent hours over the years tugging these flowers, roots and all, out of the ground and peeling open the stem to eat the white thread of pulp

Fireweed in bloom.

inside of it. I passed summer afternoons playing "he loves me, he loves me not" with the numerous purplish pink petals. After a fire, there those flowers would be in all of their bright glory in the heart of the charred landscape. They were everywhere. How could a flower so common be so special? I suppose simply because it was there with me all those years. It was there with me, doing life, a permanent and colorful stamp on my memories.

Now as an adult and a mom, I see the land and the beauty more clearly. I can appreciate what I grew up with, and I am able to see the beauty of where I live now. I drink in the towering pine trees in my backyard every day and gaze upon the rolling hills as I drive around, running errands. I can marvel at the spring blooms and the frosted land in winter. It may not be Alaska, but it has a beauty all of its own. I guess now it's my children's turn to have no clue of their surroundings, like me those many years ago. I guess it's their time to live among the beauty and the majesty of their environment and to not see. But someday, not too far in the future, they will. They will see. Then the cycle will start all over for the beauty to be unseen by the children content to play. But there will come a time, an appointed time, when they can look back and see. And see they will, just like me, the land and all of its beauty.

# Hardcore Sibling Love

Cid and me at the BLM.

My childhood was full of even more fun and memories because I had an older brother. Yes, I wouldn't have half of the stories I do if he hadn't been involved in my life. Recently, he sent me an e-mail of things to include about growing up in Alaska. What he didn't realize was that e-mailing me would stir up my own memories of us. I remember us walking to the bus in the dead of winter with flashlights to and from school because it was dark before we got to school and dark when we got out of school. He was leading the way, and I pulled up the rear. This of course was not so he could break through the fresh foot of snow to make it easier for his little sister but rather so if anything was going to eat us from behind, it was going to eat me first.

We raced home after school in the same manner, and after piling into the house, I got to wait my turn at the stove as he made Top Ramen first and then I got to enjoy my after-school snack much later. It went on like this in so many ways in the normal big brother-little sister way. He got the snow machine first and time with the

Nintendo first (hours and hours until I finally got to play after midnight), and the list goes on.

As a kid sister, I did also benefit from my older brother. I missed all of freshman initiation because he screamed, "*Don't touch my sister!*" and they obeyed because he was a senior. Pulling up the rear on the way to school, eating Top Ramen last, and sacrificing precious video game time were worth everything for his protection. He protected me when I was chasing him around a tree and slipped into my bike handle bars, splitting my chin open. Racing to my aid, he cupped his hand under my jaw and hauled me home quick as a wink, where my mother about fainted at the sight of all the blood. He was brave and determined and did what had to be done. My mom drove me in to the clinic, and I got four stitches and a scar on my chin as a reminder.

He piled me on the back of our snow machine after we idiotically went tubing down suicide hill behind our house at the pump station and flew fifty feet (maybe not that far, but as a child, it sure felt like it) in the air, crashing at the bottom and landing on a patch of ice. I landed on my back and compressed two vertebrae, and Cid slid down the hill on his face, incriminating him with scratches everywhere. Now, in hindsight, he probably shouldn't have moved his injured sister, but in his junior high mind, he was saving my life, and my memory tells me he did. My mom and a neighbor made a makeshift stretcher, loaded me into the back of a station wagon, and raced off to the clinic. I couldn't walk for a week after that, and I never really went sledding again on that hill, but my brother was my hero that day—maybe not in my mom's eyes, but he certainly was in mine . . . even though he was on the tube with me that day and probably made me go down the hill with him.

He took time off of work to pick me up from my place of employment one summer (I was in high school by this time) when my parents weren't around, for another trip to the clinic. I had cut my leg open on broken glass, and he zipped right over in his Datsun 210 (the very one we drove up to Alaska in, it was now his precious car) and sat in the clinic with me for yes, more stitches. He then headed back to work, and so did I.

I always knew I could call on my brother, and I knew that he would be there. Things haven't changed much since those days back in Tok. Well, maybe a little. He wouldn't put me in the back to get eaten anymore, and he'd probably offer me a bowl of Top Ramen first. He'd suggest we play video games together, insist we both have a snow machine to zoom around on side by side, and of course, he'd still come to my rescue. That is what I call hardcore sibling love.

Cid and me outside our house on a snow bank.

# Trusty Transportation

My mom, Marsha, and my brother, Cid, in front
of the Tok Community Center.

Our main mode of transportation as children was our bikes. Maybe other kids growing up in the eighties can profess the same thing, but truly and really in our small town of Tok, having a bike was a matter of summer survival. How else were we going to get to work? During my growing-up years, it wasn't *if* you were going to work in the summer but *where* you were going to work. Summertime was Tok's boom time, and almost every working-age kid in Tok was employed. Most of our parents worked full-time, too, and that left us kids in need of transportation.

I started babysitting at a young age and then got my first "real" job at Mukluk Land in the sixth grade. By this time, we had moved out of the BLM pump station and into government housing situated about two miles outside of town. All of my summer jobs were at least two miles away, so my trusty old bike got me there. I had a mile to bike down a dirt road, and once I hit the highway, I had at least another mile to go, so I was grateful for the bike path along the way for that last stretch of my ride. It had quite a few bumps in it from fireweed pushing through it to seek light, but it was a sight better than eating the dust that cars kicked up on the long gravel road.

Growing up, I didn't even think of asking my parents for a ride to my job. Why would I do that? I had my ride. During my high school years, I worked as a house-keeper at the Golden Bear and then at the Westmark, where my brother was a cook. My trusty old bike got me there. If I wanted to go get a movie at Eska Trading Post during the day or at night (remember it was light all the time in the summer) or was hankering for a candy bar from one of the local grocery stores, Saveway or Frontier Foods, you guessed it. My trusty old bike got me there.

My bike took me to the basketball courts (and yes, we balanced our basketballs under one arm and pedaled miles to and from town like that), and my bike got me to the school playground to meet up with friends. My bike got me to Tastee Freez so I could share a banana split with someone. Anyone.

My bike got me to Fast Eddy's for pizza and Northstar Laundromat to spend my hard-earned quarters at the arcade. Most importantly, though, my bike got me to my friends, wherever they might be. Our bikes made the difference between having summer employment and summer entertainment or simply having none. We were in most respects like other kids in America; our compass just pointed farther north.

# Visiting Family and Family Visiting

# Summer Vacation

Me, my dad, and my cousin Nancy on their family
farm in Wisconsin.

Almost every year, we packed up our suitcases for the long trip "outside" to the Lower 48. It was no small feat to get out of Tok, and what a treat it was to go to the land where, in the summer, it got dark at night and our skin got tan in the day. Many of us local kids had family that lived far away, and it wasn't unusual at all for one of us to go missing for a couple of weeks each summer, visiting all the relatives. It was a part of life, a part of growing up in Alaska.

The trip started out with a four-hour drive to Fairbanks, where we caught a flight to Anchorage. From there we flew on a red-eye flight to Seattle. Then, after maybe a lengthy layover, we flew over to Minneapolis, Minnesota, where we finally grabbed a hopper plane to a small Wisconsin airport. This was our final destination. Aside from a thirty-minute car ride to Grandpa and Grandma's, we had finally made it.

Quite often, we would spend a week in Stevens Point, Wisconsin, chasing fireflies, swimming in a city pool, and playing hide-and-go-seek with our faraway cousins in the cool, dewy grass in the night lit only by those fascinating bugs, with the glowing and blinking backsides. The darkness was a marvel for us Alaskan-raised kids.

After our week in Wisconsin, we drove to Iowa, to see my dad's side of the family, where the heat kept us up at night in my grandparents' upstairs bedroom without air conditioning, and we dined on New Albin bologna and drank innumerable ounces of Spring Grove soda pop. We frolicked and played on our uncle's farm by picking strawberries (and eating them) and then cooled off in the muddy creek that wound its way around the outskirts of the cornfields. It was riddled with rusty broken cans and drop-offs. . . . What were our parents thinking?

It was a different world down in the States, and it was every bit a part of my memories of growing up a child of Alaska. Summer vacation was a time for my parents to put up their feet, relax, and catch up with the family we had left behind on our great northern adventure. My dad always sported his Alaska t-shirts, and my brother and I made good use of our swimsuits every day. We marveled at how much all the cousins had grown and changed in just one year, and we caught up on life and news with loved ones we saw too few and far between.

Then all too soon, our visit would be done and back we would go on our long journey home. We arrived home tired, yet invigorated, sun-kissed, happy, and full of stories to tell our friends. We came home ready for another year in Alaska.

# Playing Tourist

My dad and me.

Every once in a while, we got the chance to play tourist in our great state. When you are living day in and day out in Alaska as a kid, you do take for granted the majestic mountains literally in your backyard and the other wonders of the world situated around the state—things the outside world only dreams of seeing. But when family came from thousands of miles away, making the long and expensive trip to see us, well . . . then we put on our tourist hat and boots and started walking (actually, driving hundreds and hundreds of miles would be more accurate). In fact, that was one of the things that my relatives couldn't believe: the vastness of the land and the distance between towns.

Uncle Mike, Mom, me, and Dad on the *Riverboat Discovery*.

Our usual tourist route would take us to Fairbanks, where we'd board the *Riverboat Discovery*. I was always fascinated with the marriage of the Chena and Tanana rivers as our sternwheeler paddled along its merry way. Peering over the side of the boat, you could see the muddy Tanana River meet with the clear-flowing Chena River. The stark difference between the rivers was captivating and mesmerizing. The stop at the Chena Indian village was a beautiful sight to behold. The Athabascan Indians gave tourists a glimpse into living off the land that even for us locals was special to see. I fondly remember staring at the strings of smoked salmon hanging in the trees and a man giving me a taste of the fish. On one of the tours, my aunt and uncle met the dog musher Jane Shields, who was there with her puppies. What a delight for them to meet an Iditarod racer.

After the riverboat ride, we would stay overnight in Fairbanks and watch a movie in an actual theater because even if my relatives watched one every weekend where they were from, we sure didn't get to in Tok! One of my cousins remembers that on her one trip to Alaska, we did a round-trip to Fairbanks. We left Tok around four o'clock in the morning so we could stop in at the dentist, grocery store, mall, and theater. Then, heading back to Tok, we stopped in at Delta Junction for some Pizza Bella for a late-dinner, putting us back in Tok around midnight. She couldn't believe we had to travel four hours one way to shop and that we would do a trip like that in one day. On top of that, we crammed in a movie, and it wasn't a matinee; it was in the evening and we still had to drive back to Tok! Things she took for granted, she soon saw, were things that were few and far between for us.

Me and my cousin Tricia at Denali National Park.

Our next destination was Denali National Park. Thankfully, we did often get to see that massive piece of rock, which is not always the case. One time we stayed in rustic cabins just outside the park and ate sourdough pancakes, a novelty for our out-of-state guests. There were never any guarantees that the mountain would be out, but, for us, the mountain was out (except the time my dad's parents went), and so were the bears, the caribou, the sheep, the wolves, the eagles . . . you get the picture. It's pretty great when even as a kid, you don't mind being dragged around by your parents, grandparents, aunts, and uncles to see the local sights of your state.

We also made the trip to Homer when my mom's side of the family was visiting because my mom had two cousins from Wisconsin who lived there. On our trip to Homer with my mom's parents, we stopped to picnic along the way. Grandma had packed a cooler full of summer sausage, fruit, rolls and licorice sticks (just like she did for us in Wisconsin). Down from our picnic table on the beach were people digging for clams. That was something else for my grandparents. They had never heard of such a thing. Digging for clams? Later on, we did just that.

Cid, Mom, and me clam-digging in Homer, Alaska, at Clam Gulch.

Me in front of Marly's cabin in Homer. No electricity
and no running water.

In Homer, we stayed at my mom's cousin, Marly's, home. Her cabin had no electricity and no running water, which meant the creek was the ice box and the A-frame outhouse was the bathroom. Tucked down into the lush woods, the scent of the air was keenly clean, with only the noise of the wind through the branches and the quiet whisper of the freezing creek cutting itself through her land beyond the cabin. A far cry from city life.

During our stay, we took time to tour the town and traversed the famous Homer spit. The spit is a piece of land that extends out into the ocean. You can drive on it and access the harbor, as well as eat at restaurants. Marilyn was my mom's other cousin who lived in Homer. Her boyfriend had a boat called *The Walrus*, so one day, he took us out on that cold gray ocean to the Saltry to eat. That was something even I as a kid thought was pretty cool. Boating to a restaurant? On the way, we passed Puffin Rock (I don't know if that was the rock's real name; I just remember so many puffins!), and from that time forward, my favorite bird ever, even to this day, has been the puffin.

Leaving Homer, we'd make the long trip back to Tok, stopping off in Anchorage for the night. Proving our point to the relatives that Alaska was a small place, contrary to the vastness of the land, at Chuck E. Cheese's, we ran into some old Montana neighbors who were now living in Kodiak. They too were on vacation. Alaska truly is a small world.

Anchorage was the beginning of the last leg of our trip, so it was onward and forward for another six or so hours to home. We wouldn't just drive straight through to Tok, though. A stop at the Matanuska glacier lookout site was essential, and lunch at Eureka Lodge for the best bacon cheeseburgers ever to fuel us until the end of our journey was a must. Gazing upon Gun Site Mountain and all of the spectacular views along the Glenn Highway at the Eureka Summit was remarkable if the weather was cooperating. We would arrive home a little travel weary but laden down with memories and various tourist-trap items. I got a stuffed animal (a puffin) that cost my parents an arm and a leg from a gift shop in Homer, my aunt got a pair of gold nugget earrings, and my grandpa got an Exxon Valdez oil spill hat. They may have even picked up some moose nugget swizzle sticks. Really, playing tour guide to out-of-state family was not a hard job at all. It was truly a most welcome part of my childhood.

# Faraway Family in Tok

Cid, grandma, mom, and me, holding my cabbage patch kid, standing in front of Santa Claus House, North Pole, Alaska.

Not only did we play tourist around the state of Alaska, but we also spent good quality time in Tok with out-of-state guests. First they had to fly all the way to Anchorage or Fairbanks from Wisconsin or drive from Iowa (my dad's parents didn't like to fly). One time, my grandma from Wisconsin packed fireworks in her suitcase (those were the days of plane travel) for a special treat for the kids, not realizing that it was truly daylight all day long. It's one thing to be told that it is light all of the time, and another thing to experience it. Needless to say, my grandparents took a few days of adjustment regarding the daylight and even a few days of mental adjustment regarding the weather. My grandma was shocked that it was 87 degrees when they landed in Fairbanks. Wasn't Alaska cold all of the time?

If family was coming from Anchorage, it was a little bit more of a journey to Tok. In their eyes, the land kept going on and on, and so did the highway. Along the way, my uncle couldn't get over the bush planes parked next to cars outside restaurants and businesses. Especially, since before they left Anchorage, they happened to take in the blustery wind and ocean of Turnagain Arm where people that day were wind-surfing with beluga whales. Eventually, after watching salmon swim upstream at one of the stop-offs along the highway, they arrived in Tok.

Most family landed in Fairbanks, however, so, after meeting them at the airport, picking up luggage, grabbing lunch, and stopping at Santa Claus House in North Pole, we were finally on our way home. I imagine it was almost like visiting another country for them. For us, however, it was just how it was.

It was especially meaningful when family came to visit us in Tok, instead of us visiting them down in the Lower 48. It allowed us to show family where and how we lived and allowed them to experience life as we knew it. Just knowing that after they left, our family could picture where we lived made us feel closer and more connected to those we were separated from. After they had visited, when we talked to faraway family on the phone about our town or things we were doing, they could picture us in our home. They could picture us at our school. They could picture us in our town. They could picture us in Alaska.

Their thoughts on Tok were all about the same. It was a small community, and the distance was very far between towns, which made it very isolated. My aunt marveled at the fresh air of Alaska, while my uncle was impressed with the flowers and the growing season. Going to Alaska, he had not expected things to be growing so richly, but Alaska proved him wrong. Instead of a barren wasteland, he found a place teeming with an abundance of growth and life because of the hours and hours of daylight. My cousin, who grew up outside of a small city in Wisconsin, was surprised we could bike into town from our house. She was also surprised that we had ice cream. She had imagined that where we lived, we wouldn't have such delicacies. We played croquet under the midnight sun and went swimming in a lake fifteen miles from home, and to say it was a little bit cold in the water for my cousin was an understatement. Back where she came from, you'd jump in the lake and warm up to the water. When she jumped into Moon Lake, she popped right out and headed back onto the shore. After that, she was in jeans and a sweatshirt and everyone else was in shorts and tank tops. Life was different way up north.

Activities in Tok with the relatives were plenty much to their surprise. At the time my aunt and uncle visited, my dad had a wounded owl in a dog kennel at our house. The owl had gotten hit by a car, and my dad was nursing it. The owl didn't make it, but seeing Dad nurse the owl gave my aunt and uncle a taste of his job in Alaska. We went blueberry picking up by Chicken and ate mad trapper pizza at Fast Eddy's. My mom and aunt road bikes into town on the gravel (which she remembers to be 2–3 inch rocks), and my uncle went fishing at Broken Bridge with my dad and my brother. We spent a day at Mukluk Land and sat on our deck at the house (until the mosquitoes drove us in) overlooking all of my dad and brother's antlers tied or nailed to the trees lining our driveway. My uncle had never seen such a thing. In Wisconsin, antlers would be nailed to a shed or over a garage. Even to this day, only in Alaska has he seen it done that way.

Me and Auntie Ellen posing in front of antlers.

Faraway family would come, and faraway family would go, but each time was special. Each time was a memory. Each time, a little of Alaska would go home in their hearts, and each time, a little more of them would stay in ours. Rejuvenated by the land they had seen and by the people they loved, if they could come again, they would, though I knew full well that the likelihood of that happening was slim. But I could always hope they would visit again someday, and that was good enough for me.

# Northern Holidays

# Easter

Walking down to the Tok River for sunrise service.

Easter was always a very special time of year for us in Alaska, not only because of our beliefs but also as a marker that spring was on its way. I'm not sure who thought of the idea to do Easter sunrise services in Tok, but I wish I could thank them. Yes, it was cold, usually freezing cold, but there was something incredibly special about gathering together and sharing the story of Christ's crucifixion and resurrection out in the glory of the Alaskan wilderness.

Different years had the service at different places. I remember driving out to the Tanacross airstrip overlooking the Tanana River and being all bundled up, standing with the people of Tok and surrounding areas as the blazing winter sunshine lit up the landscape in breathless glory. One time we even did an Easter egg hunt in the snow (they were plastic eggs filled with stickers) at Mike Matthews's house located next to the airstrip.

Another time, we stood on the bluffs of the Tok River by the bridge. Always afterwards we would head to the Dog Musher's, a community building where the Tok

Race of Champions dog sled races were held every year, for a giant community-wide pancake breakfast.

Easter was a community event. We may have gone to different churches or maybe not even to church at all, but that was okay. We gathered together to remember in the cold spring morning, and we ate together to fellowship in the warmth of a building because we were a community. A community ready for spring. Easter was a reflection of hope for our souls, and a reminder that spring was upon us. Although it was snowy and cold, the sun was shining (most of the time), the days were getting longer and the long, dark winter would soon be behind us. That was something we could all celebrate. That was something we could all agree upon. Spring, and the hope that came with it.

# The Fourth of July

The young ladies of Tok at the Fourth of July beauty pageant.

Even small-town girls got to do big-time events . . . like the first-ever (I think) and maybe only Tok beauty pageant. I don't know who the mastermind was behind it, but five of us lucky ladies prepared a talent and dressed up pretty for judging. I was terrified and sang into my microphone, staring at the floor. My classmate and friend Windy wrote and recited a poem in her long hot pink dress, flashing her sweet smile at the judges, which nabbed her the coveted crown. My dad was the MC, and it was held in the old Veterans of Foreign Wars (VFW) building, the same place we had our yearly Halloween party. I will never forget that evening. Beauty pageants were the stuff dreams were made of and this podunk pageant was no exception! The next day must have been the Fourth of July, because I remember riding on a float in the town parade, waving my white-gloved hand . . . a little sore that I had come in second.

The Fourth of July in Tok was a community-wide event with a large parade down the main road, mud volleyball games, and sawdust piles where we dug for half dollars, and I suppose most of us either picnicked, ran home for lunch, or grabbed a bite to eat at Fast Eddy's. One year I was on my dad's mud volleyball team with the 40-Mile Air employees. We lost, but oh, it was so much fun. We all wore matching red 40-Mile Air t-shirts and leapt, hollered, dove most ungracefully, and got super muddy. I'm pretty sure there was a softball tournament pitting the local businesses against one another too. We were like a lot of small towns that way, loving our softball, loving our community, and loving our country.

One particular year, the town headed out to Mukluk Land for an evening of fireworks. I actually worked at Mukluk Land that day because we were open late, and I remember the crowds sitting and facing the back of the park, waiting for the fireworks to go off. Around ten o'clock, the first firework shot in the air and tried as hard as it could to light up the night sky. We all knew the sky would not cooperate, however, but it didn't matter. We had fireworks! We could barely see them, but we could hear them and knew they were there. I'm sure the tourists that night got a kick out of our fireworks display—the fireworks display they couldn't see because it was daylight. But what they could see was a pretty great group of people enjoying one another and enjoying whatever living in Alaska might bring. This time it brought new meaning to watching a fireworks show . . . one you could not see but enjoyed anyway.

# Halloween

Me and my Tok classmates performing "The Broken Broomstick" for a school play around Halloween.

E very year, Halloween involved finding a fine balance of donning an amazing costume that could either survive under your snow suit or fit over it. Sometimes it was so cold, the plastic masks or plastic costumes would harden and shatter, reminding us that maybe we needed to do Halloween a little bit differently than others did. During the eighties, punk rockers were high on the costume list. We would spray our hair until it was stiff and flat with glitter or colored spray and put on bright makeup so at least our faces and parts of our hair could be seen under our hats, gloves, and coats. I don't know where we got the product. Probably on a trip to Fairbanks months earlier.

The local VFW would hold an all-invited Halloween party to go to after we had driven around town to do our trick-or-treating, our moms waiting in the warm cars so we could warm up between stops. One year my best friend, Elizabeth, and I dressed up as the California Raisins. Decked out in black tights on our legs and arms, giant brown garbage bags over our bodies (we cut leg holes in the bottom of the bag), and green-painted ponytails on the tops of our heads like stems (that stuck out of the top of the gathered garbage bag) our identities were completely hidden. With sunglasses covering our eye holes and giant cardboard red lips over our breathing holes, we kept the people guessing about who we were as we waved around our white-gloved hands.

After arriving at the party at the VFW we kids found ghoulish punch to drink, treat bags to grab, and a very mini haunted house tucked between curtains to explore. If we wanted to be grossed out after the haunted house spooked us, we could sidle up to a table set up with covered bowls. Someone would blindfold us, guide our hand into the bowls, and convince us that we were touching eyeballs, guts, and brains . . . oh my. Bobbing for apples was also a highlight, although I'm not sure why, because we all got soaked, but the most important fact was we could do all of these activities while being very, very warm inside the decorated building. What a fun time the people of Tok put on for us small-town kids.

# Christmas

Cid, Mom, Dad, and me in front of our scraggly tree.

There were always two packages that came in December that my brother and I could simply not wait to receive. Our grandma in Wisconsin took great care in shipping a box of presents along with a box of food for Christmas. She packed the food box full of Wisconsin string cheese, cheese curds (squeaky cheese), blocks of cheese, cheese spread, sausage, bags of jelly beans, homemade fudge, peanut clusters, haystacks, sugar cookies, divinity, and a can of ribbon candy. It was pure pleasure to get that box every year. Grandma knew things were hard to come by in Tok, so she made sure she packed things we could not get, plus a few VHS tapes of recorded movies like *The Breakfast Club* and *The Legend of Billy Jean*, and at least one full tape of MTV. Those prized items, those longed for VHS tapes, came in the second box. The present box.

Although the food box was extremely popular, the present box always inched ahead every year for the most exciting box of all. There were presents from the grandparents and the aunties and uncles. There were presents from the cousins and of course from Santa. After we had carefully unloaded all of our wrapped riches (and oh, the wrapping paper, all the different kinds!), the hard part came . . . the part where we put it all under the tree to sit for a few weeks until Christmas Eve, when we could open it all! There they would sit under our scraggly tinsel-tangled tree that my brother and dad had found deep in the woods behind our house. What were we to do now? The tree sat there all done up nice (with the bad side facing the wall, because every Alaska cut tree had a bad side), and the presents screamed at us from under the tree. You must have already guessed that when our parents weren't around, we shook, poked, and prodded those wrapped delicacies and slyly tore every corner until we pretty much knew what we were getting. Sorry, Mom, but true confessions are out. We were naughty, naughty children.

Finally, it would be Christmas Eve (and it felt like the evening of Christmas Eve *all* day because there were only four hours of daylight) and we could open our presents that had come out of the box (sadly, no longer a surprise). Then we'd head out for candlelight service at church, and after service, to somebody's house for dinner and good company. When we had exhausted ourselves with food and many wild hands of card games, we would head home on a very cold, very dark, and very wintry night to anxiously wait for sleep to come, because we knew in the morning came the big presents from Mom and Dad, along with stockings stuffed with an assortment of wonderful things. One year, we even found a coveted Nintendo under the Christmas tree, surely making us the envy of almost every girl and boy in town.

One memorable Christmas morning found me tearing off the wrapping paper to reveal a real Cabbage Patch Kid doll. I found out later that my grandma fought with another woman in the toy store (I think tugging and words were involved) to get the last one in stock, and yes, my grandma won. I believe she said something to the effect that her granddaughter who lived far away in Alaska needed it more than that other lady did. So that Christmas of '85, in the small town of Tok, where it was impossible to obtain such a valuable prize, I ripped open that precious commodity and loved that doll. I still love it, even today. A few years later, the local grocery store in Tok had a few Cabbage Patch Kids in stock and I bought my second one right next to the gum and candy at the checkout stand. My, how times could change in just a few years up north. Tok was moving on up. Things were becoming more and more accessible.

Looking back over the years, I realize that Christmas always was—and I pray always will be—intricately interwoven with relationship. Always. And that was how we did Christmas in Alaska when we couldn't make it down below to spend it with extended family . . . our heavenly Father reaching from above, our outside family reaching from afar, and, always, our close friends and neighbors reaching from so near.

# New Year's Eve

Heather, Becky, me, and Sandi at -70° New Year's Eve 1991.

A normal New Year's Eve for me was a potluck dinner in our church basement, board games until a few minutes before midnight, and then all of us gathering together in the main church area to welcome in the new year as we stood in a circle, grabbed one another's hands, and sang the song, "Blest Be the Tie That Binds." Then we would head back downstairs for more food and games as we kids passed back and forth through the underground tunnel that led from the church basement to the parsonage (pastor's house) basement. How is that for an Alaskan building? We didn't even have to go outside. We had our own underground tunnel that kept us warm. Parents were laughing and dealing cards, and we were chasing each other around until eventually settling down for a game of Sorry or Go Fish. Bleary-eyed but full of good food and good friends, we would head home in the dark and bitter cold to our homes to start the new year afresh.

One year, however, a few of us girlfriends decided to get together, get dressed up, make a special dinner, take a bunch of pictures, play Trivial Pursuit, and stay up all night. So we did. Donning old prom dresses and cooking up a dish of chicken tetrazzini, we laughed the night away stuck in the house because it was −70°. We braved a few pictures standing on the porch outside of the open door, and when the warm air met the cold air, we had quite the special effect for our snapshot. Laughing, we tumbled back inside to shake off the chill, never really giving another thought to the freezing weather just a few feet outside of the door. Inside was toasty warm, the wood stove was roaring merrily, and it was a very memorable way to bring in the new year. It was cold, but it was memorable.

# Small-Town Happenings

# Watermelon Days

The town of Tok showing up for Watermelon Days.
Here I am, tossing an egg.

There are some childhood memories that are so exciting and so special that thirty years later, you still tell your friends and family about them. I will never forget Watermelon Days in Tok. When I told my husband about Watermelon Days, he did not believe me. I had the proof in pictures though, and he had no choice but to accept that yes, Watermelon Days, really did occur. It happened only one time, and a good portion of the community showed up for watermelon races, egg tosses, a fire hose fight to see which team could push the watermelon across the line first—almost like a watermelon tug-of-war—and long sticks of watermelon gum handed out to us kids and adults alike. I don't know who brought the watermelons (I think a truck broke down or a plane had to land and the watermelons would spoil, so they gave them to the town), but it is something I will never, ever forget from my childhood growing up in the wilds of Alaska.

Watermelon races!

# The Circus Comes to Town

I don't have a picture. I wish I had a picture to prove it. A circus did come to Tok. That's right, a circus. It set up right by the Tok Lodge, and it was the most miserable little circus, but the most exciting thing to happen in Tok in a while. We could pay $5.00 to sit on an elephant and then pay another $5.00 for a ride on the elephant. They would lead you around in a tight little circle that took approximately ten seconds. It took longer to get on the elephant and off the elephant than to ride the elephant. What a racket! Parents had to travel through the gauntlet of cheap toys crying out to be bought to even enter the sagging, dark tent. Once inside the tent, my dad did buy us peanuts for $5.00 a bag as we sat in the stands, and when we opened them up, we found three peanuts (still in their shells) in the bag. Three.

The tightrope walker was three feet off the ground, and she kept falling off. It was pure chaos, as several acts were attempting to perform at once . . . and attempting is a generous word. I could have been in that circus. I have no idea how much my parents paid for those tickets, but whatever it was it was entirely too much, even if they were free. Nevertheless, that circus was awfully special for me as a child. I guess that memory is priceless . . . even if the circus was not.

# Summer Camp

Shen Bible Camp. I'm sitting cross-legged under the sign.

Summertime in Alaska wasn't complete without a trip to Shen Bible Camp. We kids loaded up and headed out to a place quite remote even for our standards. Parking on the highway, we'd pile into an eight-wheeled ATV and then travel through the backwoods and muck to where land ended and water began. We had to boat into the camp.

Shen Bible camp was started around 1977 or 1978. Local Tok residents Wayne Eames and Mike Matthews somehow happened upon an old mining exploration camp off the Taylor Highway and were able to purchase it for a dollar. Yes, one dollar. That was how Shen was born. It came with cabins and a cook shack. Not too shabby a deal for a camp on a lake with buildings already in place.

Those original mining camp cabins were what we bunked in. One year, when my cousin traveled to Alaska, she spent a night out at Shen with me to help out that year's staff and campers. We wanted her to have a real Alaskan experience. The two of us went out and helped with the camp duties. My dad took us down to the

Me and Cid, in front of one of the Shen cabins.

Stuck hauling gear to the boat to take to Shen.
Photo courtesy of Paul Kelley.

waterfront, where he shot off his rifle to let the people at Shen know we were ready to be picked up by the boat. Tricia and I then threw ourselves into being good helpers at the camp. Mostly, we helped in the kitchen with meals. She remembers a particularly frozen block of cheese that had been stored in the cooler buried in the ground on top of the permafrost. It hadn't had time to unthaw and she couldn't cut it without it crumbling to bits. How strange for her to have to heat up the cheese in order to melt it for grilled cheese! We helped alongside other Tok people and SEND International missionaries. It was a joint effort to ensure that the campers had the best time.

When we went to Shen, we ate really great food, got eaten alive by mosquitoes, played capture the flag, canoed to the island in the middle of the lake for an overnight stay, and got eaten alive by some more mosquitoes, and the whole time, we never, ever took a shower. Swimming in the lake did not count. In fact, it made it worse. Did I mention we got eaten alive by mosquitoes?

The highlight of our time, though, was the ice cream drop. Over the years, it was done by different pilots and different planes, but every year, the good Lord above would supply someone to drop us kids some ice cream in the lake. Someone would paddle out to pick up the package as it bobbed along gently, waiting patiently for its retrieval. It was the time of our lives, and we kids will never, ever forget Shen.

The plane getting ready to drop ice cream in the lake for the campers! Photo courtesy of Paul Kelley.

# School Times

# A Community of Teachers

Me and Cid.

I n Alaska back in the eighties, we didn't really do first-day-of-school pictures. I'm pretty sure my mom had to mail film somewhere to get it developed. I can testify that Tok did not have a One-Hour Photo. I don't even know if you could buy film in town. You probably could, but it most likely cost more than you wanted to pay.

Being absorbed in back-to-school activities as a mom now made me think back on my own school days. We moved to Alaska in March. If you live or have lived in the interior of Alaska, you know that there is still a lot of snow and there is still a lot of cold. I was in the first grade, and Mrs. Schutt was my new teacher. I stood in the doorway the morning my mom brought me in, and I stared at the children sitting at their desks. Out of the big windows looking over the side yard and onto the street, I saw mounds of snow. In the classroom on the floor, I saw mounds of boots. I don't think one child had their boots on as they sat in their seats, swinging their dampened socked feet back and forth. I simply stared. One did not do that in Montana, or one would get in trouble. I already liked my new school. My mom commented later that everybody looked a little wild and scruffy, and it wasn't long until my brother and I did too. We fit in quite nicely after a couple of months.

The next year, I sat in my second-grade classroom with Mrs. Hebert and sometimes looked longingly across the hall at the kindergarten room where Mr. Wothke taught. (He wore a beret and drove a Porsche . . . in Tok, of all places!) Oh, how I wished I had gotten to be in there. Why hadn't we moved when I was in kindergarten?! They had chickens! Real chickens! Chickens that hatched and peeped even though it was cold outside. I had missed out.

Third grade was when I mastered multiplication, and it was all because of Mr. Jacobs. He had a drawer full of candy . . . and it wasn't just any candy. It was full-sized Tangy Taffy bars. Grape. Strawberry. Watermelon. I know there was other candy in there, but that taffy was all the motivation I needed. I was a times-table champion in no time. To this day, I credit my memorization of multiplication to him. I am forever in his debt.

In fourth grade (and later sixth grade), Ms. Culver was our teacher. In her classroom, I learned how to play Oregon Trail on the computer. On April Fool's Day, she wasn't even mad when we dropped chocolate Hershey kisses in her coffee. We'd probably be suspended today, but back then . . . well, it was okay. We would stop by her house sometimes on the weekend to say hi, which I am sure she loved. I say that sarcastically. But that is what happens when you teach in a small town in the interior of Alaska. We kids knew where everybody lived, and we weren't afraid to bike up to someone's door to say hello.

When I tumbled into fifth grade, I was definitely moving up in the world. I was almost at the halfway point of the school building. The school was arranged with kindergarten through seventh grade running up to the office. Beyond the office was eighth grade through high school. Yes, every single kid in one school. What I remember most about fifth grade was Ms. Forsmark. She was gone the year I was in fifth grade, so Mrs. Lancaster (such a sweet lady) was my teacher, but I have to mention Ms. Forsmark because she was known for her recess-duty line-up call. She didn't use a whistle. She didn't need one. With her hand cupped around her mouth and a strong, clear voice, she would shout out into the Alaska wind and cold, "Liiiiiiiiiine uuuuuuuupp," signaling the end of recess, and we would. Some of us girls would crowd around her and help her holler it. She also looked the other way at recess sometimes when we huddled in the hockey shed, trying to get warm. Eventually, she would kick us out, but when it was almost –20°, she did have some compassion.

Me posing for basketball pictures.

I hit the ground running in sixth grade, and I hate to say it, but it was a blur. Sorry, Ms. Culver; I should remember more. I really should. I started basketball and began traveling with the team while also being a cheerleader. I had the most amazing poodle perm one could ever wish for. How is that for my memories? They are all about the sports and the hair.

After the bad perms and shiny silky hand-me-down uniforms for basketball, I must say that my most life-changing year was seventh grade. There, I discovered my passion for writing. By this time, we were changing classes for each subject, and Mr. Persson was my English teacher. He loved English and made English fun. We wrote stories in class, watched plays like *Romeo and Juliet* on the TV rolled into the room, and wrote biographies about our classmates. Mr. Persson wrote one about Stephen Dartt and called it "The Red-Tipped Dartt," which I thought was brilliant, since Stephen was a redhead. I wrote a story called "The Dream" that I read in front of my class. I was encouraged to enter it into the talent fair that was coming up in the district, so I did. I ended up winning a first-place trophy. Mr. Persson is my earliest recollection of my discovery of what I love to do today: write.

In the eighth grade, the beloved Mr. Kelley retired. Why, right before me?! Everyone looked forward to the high school graduation of the kids who had been in Mr. Kelley's eighth-grade class. He video-recorded every eighth-grade student reciting the Declaration of Independence, and then, four years later, he played it for the whole school and town to see. They had been children, it seemed, on that VHS tape, but now, they were on the verge of adulthood.

It all turned out okay for me, even though Mr. Kelley was retired when I got to eighth grade. I saw Mr. Kelley all of the time anyway, but I am still a little distraught even today that he exited right when I knew I was going to be his star pupil. He would probably jokingly say he retired because he saw me coming!

Finally, I made it to high school. Oh, the glory. I was already 100% into band with Mr. Ramponi, who demanded excellence, so excellence was what he got. The music program in Tok was fantastic. We had a strong concert band and jazz band, and eventually, we had a choir. We often took first place in regionals and went to the state music festival in Anchorage. What a pleasure to play with other students who worked hard at their instruments! How in the world did we end up with a class-act musician in Tok for a teacher? I don't know how, but we did. We were very, very fortunate.

The music program also put on what was known as the jazz band dinner dance. When you live in a little town in the middle of nowhere, you kind of have to make your own entertainment, and the school was often a central part of entertaining Tokites. A local restaurant catered steaks with a side of loaded baked potato, and the band played on and on. People came out not only to support the school but also to shake off a little bit of cabin fever. Under the direction of Mr. Ramponi, many kids graduated high school with a fervent love of music instilled in them.

Mr. Hather taught gym and World Geography . . . and if you couldn't, or didn't pass World Geography, I don't know what to tell you. He reviewed *everything*, even the test. If you took notes, and sort of studied, you had an easy A. Then there was gym. When I was in school, you had gym class forever, meaning you had it until you graduated. There was none of this business about needing only one credit of physical education. I was the only girl in my class at times. It was lonely running laps with boys and climbing the dreaded rope to the ceiling. You know what the safety net was? A flat one-inch padded mat and Coach Hather telling me he would catch me if I fell. Whenever one of my girl classmates returned, my sigh of relief probably could be heard up and down the school hallways. Oh, it was a lonely, lonely time for me when I was the only girl in gym class. But I still brag today that

Me waiting to play piano with the Tok jazz band during a school concert.

Jazz band dinner dance. Here I am dancing in a pink dress with my dad.

I actually know how to bowl with correct form and can hand-score a bowling game no matter how many strikes, spares, or turkeys. Mr. Hather made sure of that.

Another teacher-coach at school was Mr. Woods. Mr. Woods taught history and was my basketball coach and a local pastor (talk about a man who wore many hats!). Having a coach as a teacher helped keep your grades up when your coach knew every academic move and dangled "you won't play ball if you get bad grades" over your head. We were motivated to do well, and do well we did. Our whole team was counting on us.

I owe any knowledge of science and math, and a big chunk of good times, to Mr. Bell. He told the best stories, period. We, of course, knew how to get him talking, and boy, could he spin a yarn. But he didn't just tell stories. He taught us too, lest you think he slacked at his duties.

I remember a time when Mr. Bell got stranded out on his snow machine. It was a very scary incident. Mr. Keech (our shop teacher, and yes, I took shop in high school, and hunter's safety . . . both were required) and his son, Mark, went after Mr. Bell that night. The three of them had a trap line together that year, and they had set up a system so if the person who was running the line wasn't back by a certain time, the others would go out and check on the one who was on the line. That system saved Mr. Bell's life. I remember him sitting in his wheelchair at school because he had frostbite on his toes and taking off his socks to show all of us kids his blackened appendages.

To this day, I tell my kids to hush in the same way Mr. Bell told us to "hush" in class. He had a strong Mississippi accent, and the way he hushed us was quite effective when we were rowdy.

The list of wonderful teachers goes on and on. Ms. Ware taught me to type (thank goodness), and Ms. Young exposed me to new types of reading and confirmed my love of writing and literature. There were also substitutes (parents and such, like my mom and Mrs. Keech) who stepped in and helped us kids. The administration staff also did their best by us. Mrs. Kelley gave us a welcoming smile and constant patience as we begged to use the phone after school to make alternate plans. Mr. Hosken (the principal) kept the peace and knew each and every one of us. We were never just a number at school.

Mr. Hosken even heard out my hysterical, high-pitched ranting after I opened my locker and found two fresh dead grouse hanging in there as a nice surprise. Seriously, they had to have been shot right before school, because they were still warm. I would have held firm that they had been put there by a boy in my class by the name of Eric Cramer, if the true culprit had never stepped forward in 2014. After all of these years of me unjustly accusing Eric in my heart, Seth Donnelly, another classmate, bravely confessed it was him. He had found the freshly killed grouse on the back of Thor Jorgenson's snow machine parked in front of the school that morning, and had rigged them up in my locker for my sweet surprise. I have no idea what became of those grouse. I hope someone had a very tasty dinner.

Even Bob McCarthy, the janitor, was a staple of our schooling. An ever-present part of the school, he could be seen mopping the halls, cleaning the bathrooms, and pushing the giant push broom over the gym floor not only during school but also after basketball games. He helped boil and dye the Easter eggs for our all-school Easter egg hunt, and he didn't seem to mind us kids stopping to chat for a minute between classes. Some of the kids pulled pranks on him, and some were probably mean to him, but I can still picture him standing in our halls, seeming to keep watch over our school and each and every one of us. It's not every day that a janitor gets a yearbook dedicated in his honor, but Bob McCarthy did.

Those were the days. Some very special days. Some very special years. Several of the teachers, coaches, and administrators mentioned above have passed on from this world: Mrs. Schutt, Ms. Culver, Mr. Bell, Mr. Keech, Mr. Hosken, Coach Hather, Coach Woods, and Bob McCarthy. They may be gone, but their influence, love, care, and dedication live on in many of us kids who called Tok home. They chose to live in that little, isolated place, doing their best and giving their all for a bunch of wild and scruffy sock-only-wearing kids like me.

# Championship Games

The Lady Wolverines waiting to play
in a state championship game.

G rowing up in Alaska and playing sports went hand in hand for a lot of us. It was normal to be gone for a five-day trip as we traveled to Nenana and Su Valley, then to Anchorage and back to Tok. The teachers got all of our homework together, and our parents packed us up and put money in our pockets, and off we went. Some kids went without money in their pockets, and then the coaches and chaperones stepped in so the kids wouldn't starve. Better for a kid to be a part of something and pitch in some money than have that kid sit home in Tok and miss out simply because they had a need somebody could take care of.

Sometimes we traveled by bus the whole way, like when we made the long trek to Valdez and Homer or the not so long trip to Northway for probably the most exciting games of the year. Other times we took the ferry to Cordova or an airplane to Bristol Bay, King Salmon, or Barrow. The girls' basketball team traveled in a passenger van to Whitehorse, Canada, and the boys and girls often found ourselves playing for state championships in Anchorage. The games were held at Service

High School, a huge step up in school size from our home in Tok. We girls would enter the gym and just stare. There was the open court, with seating everywhere up into the rafters. Our little K–12 school gym had bleachers on one side and the wall on the other. How strange to stand on the court and look so far up and around. So much space. So many people.

We were in the big time now, with an announcer for our games to boot. They never got my last name, Breeser, right, so my mom would seek them out and tell them how to pronounce it. That was just a little embarrassing. I can still see our faithful Tok crowd in the stands cheering us on at those championships. They had traveled over six hours to come support us, paying out of their own pockets for hotel rooms and meals. Whatever we did as a school, we often did as a town. To this day, I still get nervous butterflies in my stomach whenever I enter a gym. The smell takes me back to the many years of playing basketball, some of the best memories from my childhood. The stories from all those bus, van, ferry and plane trips, and the faithfulness of our coaches and parents are branded on my heart. They are seared in my mind. They are present in my thoughts. It took the kids *and* the adults to make something so special not so easily forgotten.

The Lady Wolverines, 1986. I was in the sixth grade and playing
in the big leagues!

# Basketball Trips and Roadside Pit Stops

The Tok Wolverines getting ready to play.

My brother swears up and down that on long road trips for basketball games when rest stops were few and far between, the school bus would stop on the side of the road and boys would do their business on one side of the bus and girls would do theirs on the other. I truly do not remember this. Maybe it is a repressed childhood memory, maybe it never really happened, or maybe I stayed on the bus, refusing to relieve myself where a boy, or worse yet, my coach, could easily interrupt my not-so-private moment. Plus, it was freezing outside. The stress of having to go to the bathroom with many eyes watching and the added subzero temperatures made this situation insane, possibly unbelievable, and wholly and unequivocally Alaska.

What I do remember about those long road trips, however, were the Tanacross village boys playing "Rockin' Robin" over and over again on a portable boom box. We ate Doritos and Lay's baked potato chips, then washed it all down with a two-liter of Pepsi. Not Coke, Pepsi. We traveled for hours with our pillows, sleeping bags, and packed gear (and the coaches praying that we had packed all of our uniforms, because people forgot socks, shoes, jerseys . . .) until we arrived at our destination, some school somewhere in Alaska that we would call home for a day or two. We bedded down on classroom and gym floors, tucked in our sleeping bags, getting the rest of champions for our game the next morning.

Often, we'd depart from our home school on Wednesday and play Thursday, Friday, and Saturday, with a return trip home Sunday. We made the most of our gallivanting trips. Friendships were cultivated and destroyed; relationships blossomed and burned; and coaches and chaperones got another jewel in their crowns for heaven. It wasn't unusual for a Tok kid to fan the flames of romance with an opposing team player, and embark on a tumultuous, long-distance relationship kept alive only by phone calls, profession of love on our locker basketballs that were made of construction paper, and snail-mail letter writing. Then, at the end of the season, the romance would fizzle and sputter out, with a sometimes dramatic parting of ways at regionals, or the state tournament. Yes, those trips were wrought with drama. The best kind of drama. Small-town school drama. I remember how strange it was, after I moved to New Hampshire, and began playing basketball for the Mohawks, to load up the bus for an after-school basketball game at a neighboring town. What? No overnights? No airplanes? No ferries? No five-day trips? It just wasn't the same. I had been doing big-time travel since the sixth grade. I didn't know that the rest of the world did things differently. The only one-day trip I recall in Alaska was to play our rival school in Northway. Our games against the Warriors were legendary, and most of our town and their entire village showed up. Popcorn flew, refs were loved and loathed, and no matter who won or lost, it seemed nobody won or lost. Otherwise, it was on the bus for long days of travel and, apparently, side-of-the-road pit stops from there on out.

Such lively times we had, and yes, there was a reason the girls' coach had white hair. It was us, I just know it. Twenty-plus years later, memories are still carved in my mind like it's an old oak tree: I know that I was most fortunate to have lived in a time and place that wrought so many exceptional and extraordinary memories.

# The Russians

I don't know many people who can say that when they were in high school, Russia came to their town and played basketball against them. That was us, though. It was quite the event when a Russian girl's basketball team came to play the Lady Wolverines. They did not speak any English, but boy, could they play ball in their bikini-bottom shorts and flat old-school Converse shoes! We could not beat them. Several families hosted the girls, including us. Marina and Ura stayed as our guests, and even though we could not communicate, we still had normal teenage fun.

The Lady Wolverines vs. Russia

We took them out snow machining, and every day, they gave us some token of appreciation from Russia. They gifted us with postcards, pins, pens, tablecloths, shawls, and other Russian items. We in turn gave them a place to stay, food to eat, and a trip to the hair salon, and took them to the store and gave them $20.00 to buy whatever they wanted. They loved Granny Smith apples, and they also loved Pepsi. They didn't like popping open the can, though, so my mom and dad had to do it for them. They were also amazed that we had a garage door opener. It was a novelty to them, something they had never seen before.

From Tok, they traveled on to play ball in a few other places. Their star player, Julia, ended up blowing out her knee in Valdez, but Alaska fixed her up and took good care of her. I've never seen or heard from those five girls again. I probably never will. But they made a special mark on my childhood. Not everyone gets to play ball, or simply play, with their Russian neighbors.

Heather, me, and four of the Russian girl basketball players.

# Homecoming

Me dressed up for gangster day during homecoming week.

Homecoming. That one word evokes quite a large and involved memory of school for me. We may have been a little town, and we may, in some people's opinions, have had a lot of nothing, but we certainly weren't lacking in school spirit. Homecoming was one of the biggest school events of the year (besides prom), with everyone in the high school throwing themselves into a flurry of activity. Each class had a hallway to decorate, a giant poster for the gym to create, costumes for each theme day, and lunchtime pep-rally activities to win. Not only that, but we had a game to get ready for, a giant bonfire to build behind the school ice rink, and a homecoming court to vote in.

First, we had to decorate the halls. Now, this wasn't just a few posters here and there. Each class came up with a theme, and we covered the halls with paper, streamers, and various other decorations. This was no small-town shindig. This was the big time. It was almost a mini prom in the hall. Each class was judged on a point system, so nobody shirked on their hallway festivity duties. Then each class made a giant poster for the gym. Some were amazing. Some were not so amazing. I still wonder to this day when all of the work got done. I also wonder how many teachers stayed late to chaperone. I'm sure it was many.

Each year, we had different theme days, ranging from the seemingly simple spirit day to gangster day, opposite-sex day, backwards day, baby day, and more. I don't know how it goes down nowadays in the local schools, but we went all out like we were first graders on Halloween night. We were being judged for this, and we did not like to lose. I have to say that opposite-sex day was by far the most popular as high school boys teetered in the hallways on borrowed high heels and very, very short miniskirts. I doubt we learned anything in our classroom lectures that week, but the guys learned how to put on mascara, lipstick, and panty hose, so it wasn't a total waste of education. Every afternoon, teacher's tallied the points for each class. They counted up how many kids wore costumes and then had various activities during the afternoon pep-rally for us kids to earn more. We had a burping contest (which I won one year), an iron stomach contest (one of my classmates ate a Hershey's chocolate syrup-covered tomato, and another scarfed down a raw onion floating in sauerkraut and ice cream), relay races, and a hoop-shooting contest. Male teachers dressed up like cheerleaders, and things got a little bit R-O-W-D-Y.

Eventually, the week wound down, and by Friday afternoon, points were finalized, and a class was declared the winner. What did the class win? Bragging rights, I suppose. I don't remember any prize. But then again, I don't think my class ever won. The pep-rally that day was on the more serious side. The homecoming court was announced; we, the kids of Tok, were dressed in our Sunday best; and the out-of-town bus would roll in. Our opponents would enter our school with their game faces on. They would stomp the snow off their boots in our school and settle themselves in for the night, eager for the first game. It was always a packed house (homecoming or not), and with the giant posters declaring our awesomeness staring down at us and with our names and jersey numbers plastered all over the walls and lockers, we, the Tok Wolverines, were invincible. Some years we won and some years we lost, but never in my time did we lose our school spirit. After the last buzzer sounded, we showered, did up our hair, bundled ourselves up, and headed outside to watch our giant bonfire burn. Afterward, our dance wasn't formal (just our coolest jeans, shoes, and shirt) but we did the Hammer dance like nobody's business and slow-danced to every hair metal band love ballad known at that time on earth. After that, the party was over but our season was just beginning. We had the attitude of being unstoppable. Win or lose, we were Wolverines.

# Prom: One Magical Night

Me and Cid at prom, 1991.

Prom was the biggest event of the year. At least it was for me. Starting in the eighth grade, my goal was to go to prom, and as an eighth grader you could go . . . if you got picked to be a server. It was a privilege to get chosen for this duty. We not only got to dress up in fancy clothes, but most importantly, we got to be a part of something grown up and beyond. Sure we spent the night serving punch, assisting in the kitchen, and making sure everything went smoothly, but we also saw the dresses, the suits and ties, the moments, and the magic. I think I even got to dance one dance.

Of course having prom meant that we had to get our dresses and suits and ties from somewhere. Sometimes we would nab a prom dress on a basketball trip. My freshman year we were in Anchorage, at the Dimond Center Mall, and I picked up my dress, gloves, and shoes. It was months before prom but when one lives in a place where they are hours away from a mall, one had to plan ahead. Other times we would order from a catalog, or a mom would volunteer to take some of us girls to Fairbanks to go prom dress shopping. In a very focused trip, we would shop at every store until we finally landed on the dress, shoes, gloves, jewelry and nylons for our upcoming fairytale night.

In Tok, prom wasn't just for the seniors. If it was, there wouldn't be a prom. The junior class put on the prom for the senior class and all high school grades were allowed to attend. Each year, the junior class picked a theme, and then went right to work on making it the best prom possible. After all, the class coming behind them was responsible for their senior prom next year. It was best not to shirk on prom night duties.

Themes ranged from "Moonlight and Roses", "Under the Sea", "A Night to Remember", and "Stairway to Heaven". The year our class planned prom was the year Robin Hood took theaters by storm and "Everything I Do, I Do it for You" was born. I was class president that year and took it upon myself to order all of the prom paraphernalia from the thick prom catalog. We spent, or rather I spent, several thousand dollars of school funds, and we all worked hours after school and into the night (including many teachers) to pull off a medieval prom, castles and all. We even nabbed the science room skeleton to hang on the castle wall. Russ and Jan Persson, dance chaperones, rented costumes to wear adding even more enchantment to our night. It was a charmed evening. It was also the last year I would attend prom at Tok School. My girlfriends graciously snubbed dates to attend with me. I think, looking back, I made them. I could be quite persuasive, and I am regretful if I robbed any of them a chance at their dream date.

We transformed our high school gymnasium into a magical, mysterious, and miraculous place. Entering through those gym doors transported us to a new destination that was way beyond our small town and barren landscape of an Alaskan May. Gazing around at the yards of gossamer, tulle, crepe papered ceiling, disco balls, balloons, decorated tables, champagne glasses engraved with the prom theme, and the dazzling dance floor, it truly was like we had escaped to a world where happiness never ended. It was how we did prom every year.

Later, after my move out of Alaska, I attended my senior prom in New Hampshire. I was taken aback, and shocked, at how my new school did prom. What do you mean you don't decorate your gym for prom? We instead had tickets to a local, fancy resort, where we had catered dinner and danced in an elegant hotel ballroom. It was nice, don't get me wrong. In fact, it was quite swanky, glamorous, and posh. But it wasn't the magic I had come to not only look forward to, but to expect.

I'm not sure what the senior prom theme was the year I left Alaska. I could dig out an old yearbook and look. But it might just leave me feeling a little forlorn. After I returned to Alaska in 1994, for my best friend Elizabeth's graduation, my former classmates informed me, with what I hope today was humor, that I spent so much

Russ and Jan Persson, chaperones for prom, 1992.

on prom our junior year they were in debt up to their eyeballs. Now, in my defense, I had no clue I was moving at the time I placed the order. I was just making sure we put on a good prom!

Anyway, my class, the class of 1993, had to work concessions all year to pay back the school. Then, when it came time for their senior class trip at the end of the year, because of me, all the money they had earned went to pay off prom debt I had acquired for them. They ended up with an end-of-the-year class trip to Broken Bridge (a place right outside of Tok) to go fishing for the day. Fishing. Other classes went to at least Fairbanks...and some even went to Hawaii. That is a sad legacy I left for my class. I am so sorry. So, I hope the junior class made magic for them, like we did for our seniors.

# Washington, DC, and Juneau Close Up

Washington, DC, Close Up meeting with Senator Ted Stevens.

We may have lived miles from what some would call civilization, but our teachers were on the lookout for opportunity for us kids. One of those opportunities was Close Up. A group of us from Tok School plus others from around the state boarded a plane and made the long trip to Washington, DC, where cherry blossoms fluttered and warm air assaulted us. We were headed to learn about the workings of our national government.

We spent the week touring our nation's capital, seeing the sights, meeting our state legislators, touring museums, taking a cab for the first time (and getting ripped off in the process), riding on a subway for the first time, seeing homeless people and street performers for the first time, and getting to know other kids from Alaska. My heart went out to a couple of the kids in the group because the food was so disagreeable to their systems. They were used to eating their traditional foods, and the processed food from Washington made them sick for the whole trip.

My classmate, Gus Kincaid and I, went to Juneau, Alaska, the state capital, for a week to gain a greater understanding of how our state government worked. We stayed in a youth hostel, which was quite the experience. I had never even heard of a hostel until that trip. My eyes were opened to a bigger world than I had known. Sleeping in bunk beds with other kids I didn't know, waiting in line for the bathroom, eating communally, and tucking my stuff away to ward off the temptation for someone to steal, was foreign to me. Again, I felt bad for a couple of the kids visiting from around the state, this time for those who were not used to sharing bedrooms, bathrooms, and showers so they did not sleep very well or shower that week. It was a culture shock for them to be in such a populated place and in such close quarters with no privacy.

The week was spent touring our capital and sitting in on and participating in mock law-making sessions. We also visited the Juneau penitentiary (Lemon Creek Correctional) to see how the prison worked. It had a very nice gym and as we sat in the bleachers to observe the inmates I didn't know what to expect. I think I expected friendly faces because the gym was so nice, but the men in the prison sent us intimidating glances, and I realized that the people locked up there were maybe not so nice. My friend Becky (from Tok) had recently moved to Juneau. Her dad was the Director of the Division of Wildlife Conservation in Juneau. I stayed a night with her and we hiked near the Mendenhall Glacier and caught up on all the Tok gossip. It was my one and only trip to Juneau, and it was a beautiful journey on the very windy ferry to and from our state capital. It was an opportunity provided by my school district . . . an opportunity I could have never had on my own. So many of us kids saw parts of Alaska that other people only hoped to see. I would never have gone to Juneau if I hadn't been involved in student government. Same with other school sponsored trips like Seldovia, for a band trip, and all the aforementioned places (Cordova, King Salmon, Valdez, etc.) for basketball. Because many of us were involved at our school, we went, we saw, and we covered a lot of ground, experiencing a rare opportunity not offered to many.

# Bush Fashion

Me and my friend Jennifer in a prime example of Tok fashion.

Tok was the epitome of high fashion. I of course say that with tongue in cheek. Often, I have told my kids that growing up in the great far north put me around ten years behind everyone else in America, hence the reason my 1993 senior pictures looked more like 1985. It was bush wear at its finest, and I grew up thinking that every male in high school wore heavy metal t-shirts every day and that rat tails were a necessary commodity for everyone, boys and girls alike. You couldn't buy clothes in Tok unless you counted Wadsworth's (they had a pile of work jeans) or a mail-order catalog, and who was going to pay shipping for that? We made back-to-school shopping treks to Fairbanks for a weekend of stocking up at Lamonts, Jay Jacobs, and, if we were super lucky, the Brass Plum at Nordstrom's. Mind you, these trips happened only a couple of times a year.

Those trips were a huge highlight of my life. We'd stay in a hotel, usually the Captain Bartlett, and we'd eat at McDonald's. What a treat! After hours of shopping, we'd head home with all of our school clothes for the year. Every kid had

Air Jordan's for basketball or Reebok Pumps, and we all had some type of acid-washed something—usually jeans, but a fashionable few had jean jackets. I sported an Esprit bag every year for my book bag and had at least two Swatch watches on at all times. B.U.M. equipment was included every other day in my wardrobe (and everybody else's), and if you didn't own a Spuds MacKenzie t-shirt (or two or three or four), then seriously, you weren't from "around here." The popular girls wore Keds, and if you didn't have your hair poodle-permed and sun-glitzed . . . well, you just weren't Tok cool. Oh, and for goodness sakes, peg those pants, or else face cynical laughter in the halls. Mind you, pegging had already gone out of style elsewhere years before, but guess what? We didn't know that in Tok, and what mattered most of all was Tok fashion standards, which really weren't standards at all.

# Friendship

My seventh grade class at Eagle Trail Campground.

Often, when people ask me where I grew up and I tell them Alaska, they follow it up with the question "Where in Alaska?" I usually get two responses. If the person isn't familiar with Alaska and I tell them Tok, they stare at me too long and finally admit they have no idea where that is. If the person is familiar with Alaska and I tell them Tok, they stare at me too long and finally say, "I'm sorry." I always laugh and tell them that I'm not sorry, it was a great place to live.

Back when I was a kid, there was no Internet to get lost in and no cell phone to get absorbed with, and video games were just starting to emerge as a total time waster for kids. We got lost in, absorbed with, and wasted time with our friends. It seemed like every minute of every day for me was about being with friends. Whether it was riding the bus to school, meeting at lockers between classes, congregating at lunch tables in the gym, crowding together in a little group at recess, practicing basketball as a team, hanging out after homework, or coordinating sleepovers every single free Friday night of the year, life was always and continually about friends.

We'd plan late-night movie marathons, daytime gravel-pit snow machine parties, and Flexible Flyer sledding engagements outside town limits (down mostly abandoned steep, icy roads). I wasn't focused on the mountains in my back yard or the moose in my freezer or the snow sneaking over the tops of my boots. I was focused on the people in my life, and the most important people at that time were my friends. We rode four-wheelers all over town in the summer, tried on all our new clothes together for school in the fall, froze our toes while ice skating at lunch recess in the winter, and waded in freezing-cold puddles every spring thaw. We were connected by our remote life, not just for that time but also into today and tomorrow and the next day after that.

There is a flame of friendship that burns strong in the hearts of the children of the north that has not been extinguished by time or distance. Although many of us have moved to different cities, states, or even countries, the memories and experiences of our youth in Alaska keep us bound in a time and place that we can call uniquely ours. Those years of time invested in each other, the years we got lost in friendship and thoroughly absorbed with people, have resulted in ties that exist even to this day. Our shared life made shared memories, which made our shared bond. Our shared bond of friendship.

# School Memories

Boarded-up Tok School.

S chool was my life as a kid. It was my excitement, my social outlet, and my something to do while living in the interior of Alaska. Most of my childhood memories revolve around the days and hours spent in our K–12 school. It wasn't unusual that as an elementary kid, I knew who the seniors were and they knew me. My days were filled with learning from committed teachers and spending time with my friends. I recall leaving campus at lunch to take the trail to the local store to buy potato wedges or slushies. We kids played caribou at recess on the school front lawn. We would all line up on one side of the front schoolyard (we were the caribou), and then one to two people were the wolves in the middle. We caribou had to run across the yard and not get caught by a wolf or we died and turned into wolves. The last caribou standing won.

Because there was no school lunch provided, we gathered together in the gym or outside, sharing whatever our moms had packed that day. When the last day of the school year was upon us, we all—yes, every single grade—picked up the trash around town and then met up at the new future school site (we did this for years before the new school was built) for a huge picnic with games and a lively water balloon fight, teachers included.

After I moved the summer right before my senior year to New Hampshire, I attended a high school that had fifty kids in my graduating class . . . more than had been in the entire high school I had just left behind! I have to admit I had a little culture shock. There were no little kids filing down the hall for me to tease, and everyone in New Hampshire ate hot lunch in an actual cafeteria. Except me. I still brought my lunch . . . eating cafeteria food was just too much change. There was no recess and no open campus, and when the end of the year came, I wondered why we didn't clean up the town, and I wondered where my big picnic was. But after all was said and done, I was able to remember home and appreciate what I had left behind.

My ticket home. The message on the back said, "To Niki we give a plane ticket, to Alaska because you miss it. Just remember us in New Hampshire, and stop in some time for a visit."

As I graduated in a town far, far away from really the only school I had ever known, I was able to stand on stage and look at my new friends, who had welcomed me with wide, open arms. For a graduation gift, my class gave me a fake plane ticket back to Alaska, because they knew I missed it so much. One thing I knew as I walked up to the microphone to give my graduation speech, was that I was on an adventure, and on that adventure, I had no regrets. I would never have come to know the people surrounding me at that moment if I hadn't moved to New Hampshire. Maybe it took pulling up roots from Alaska for me to finally see what a great adventure I had been living. No matter what awakened my heart, that heart is still adventurous today. Since then, I have stood on my stage of life in Idaho, Washington and Texas. Each place has surrounded me with people I would have never known if I hadn't said yes to adventure and the path God set before me. Living in Alaska prepared me in so many ways, to live life well, to live life to the fullest, and to live life with no regrets. Alaska was a good teacher, and like a good student, I was taught.

# Community

# Belonging and Being

Mom, Blair, and Nancy.

I f I ask myself what are the top impressions I have of growing up in Alaska and I don't allow myself to think on it deeply, the images that fly through my mind are the mountains, the town itself, and all the people surrounding me. Tok residents were a part of everyday life. We were in the store together, picking up mail at the post office together, attending church together, or simply passing each other on the road during the year. The people were also a part of my school life. They were there clapping at school concerts, judging entries at the annual talent show, and cheering all of us on at our sporting events. Even after our games or matches, they sought us out to encourage us, pat us on the back, congratulate us, or console us.

For me, Tok wasn't just a blip on the map for tourists to stop at and stay over in the summer. It was my community. It was my family. It was my home. Long after the visitors had gone for the summer, we were still there. We were living. We were surviving. We were thriving. We were growing deeper as a community, and we kids were simply growing up.

The people of Tok played numerous roles in my life (and the lives of all the other kids at school), and they wore many different hats. My teachers were also my coaches. They were my parents' friends, so we had dinner and lunches and even holidays together. They taught my Sunday school. They drove my bus in the morning and afternoon and then rented me movies in the evening from the store that they owned. They were everywhere, all around me. That was my normal.

The isolation of our community during winter months and the events that brought in surrounding communities (even more far reaching) were what helped foster the closeness and togetherness of our town. If we had some type of basketball tournament like a round robin or even the state regional basketball or wrestling tournament, the people of Tok were there. They were there to pay admission, buy concessions, and cheer on "their" kids. We were their kids. We were important. We were Tok.

We were Tok because of the people, not because of the highway, gift shops, campgrounds, hotels, or restaurants. Those buildings would have been nothing and the highway would have led to nowhere without the people. We were Tok because of the community, not because of the tourists or because we were the first major stop on the Alaska Highway. We were Tok because of us. Without us, there would have been no town. Without the people who lived there . . . well, it just wouldn't have been Tok.

# The People

Me and Wayne Eames, a resident of Tok and part
of our church Faith Chapel.

N o matter which way I look at it, I just can't (and maybe I don't want to) get
around it: Living in Alaska will always and wholeheartedly be about the
people, not just the location. Did I see majestic mountains clothed in snowy splen-
dor? Yes, I did. Did I see graceful caribou and their young meander across the Alcan
Highway? Yes, I did. Did I gaze in wonder at a sun dog piercing my eyes in the dead
cold of winter? Yes, I did. I saw northern lights that would put any man-made form
to shame, and I stumbled upon tundra roses that were clothed in more beauty than
any young Hollywood starlet could ever hope to be. I gazed upon soaring bald
eagles high overhead and down upon salmon fighting their way upstream. I saw

ptarmigan waddling across the road in their winter white wardrobe. I experienced the sun on my face in the dead of night during summer, and the bitter, burning, blustering cold wind stinging my cheeks during the height of winter. Yes, I saw these things and experienced these things, but still to this day, what wraps around me close and holds me tighter than a perfectly made mukluk are the arms of the Alaskan people that held me.

Oh sure, there were some people who came and went (eventually, I was one of them). Mostly, I am talking about the wanderers and those who worked in Tok just for the summer. But when the tourist season ended and our little town settled down to our 1200 or so residents, we really were in a place where everyone knew our names. And in that place with those people was where the arms of Alaska found me. Those arms cheered me on during basketball games and hung around to congratulate me or offer condolences afterward. Those same people and their arms clambered to the gym during school concerts to listen attentively, clap wildly, and support generously. Business owners extended their arms to offer summer jobs to us kids when the school year wound to a close. Arms held me close after church just because they could. Arms hugged me tight on my birthday because they were so glad to know me. Arms said well done at the end of the school year because they had invested in me. Arms reluctantly released me and said good-bye when we moved away, because they loved me. The arms of Alaska held me then, and the arms of Alaska still hold me today.

# Unique Opportunity

An ariel view of the town of Tok, 1988.

I n the eyes of some, we kids didn't have as many opportunities as other kids because we grew up nestled in the remote interior of Alaska. In fact, I've even said that to people at times myself. There were no local swimming pools for swim lessons and no dance centers for dance lessons. Our organized sports options were only during the school year. We had basketball, cheerleading, volleyball, wrestling, and hockey. There was no football, soccer, golf, lacrosse, baseball, softball, or anything else, unless you counted gym class. There was no YMCA. You could go to some pretty amazing sports camps and music camps in the summer if you had time and money to travel to Fairbanks or Anchorage or even out of state.

Because we were lacking in after-school and summer programs, I would wager to say that if an outsider were looking in, they might say raising your child in Tok meant raising them with limited opportunity. That, however, is entirely based on how you look at it. Through the backward-looking eyes of an adult child of Tok, I would have to disagree and say that our place of growing up was ripe with opportunity that maybe we learned to truly appreciate only after we were grown and gone. A combination of the people, the time, and the place made it a perfect storm of wonderful . . . wonderful opportunity.

I think we Alaskans who lived in Tok during the eighties and early nineties were there at a very favorable and rare time. The people during that window created circumstances that made it possible for us to do some really great things. Whether it was our top-notch band director who whipped us into musical miracles or our high-quality teachers and coaches who taught us skills that enriched our lives and made us winners many times over, we had opportunities with people . . . people whom today I still unequivocally respect and feel deeply connected with. At that time, we had very little television, and maybe even less radio. We were a people who met face to face and found that our land and our small town were our playground. We slept under the midnight sun, watched buffalo and moose migrate through our backyards, and called our neighbors at all hours of the night to watch the never-tiring northern lights. Our lives were peppered with outdoor activities in the summer and hanging out with friends at their houses when the temperatures plummeted in the winter. We had community potlatches and dinners throughout the year. If you belonged to a church, every holiday offered potlucks, singing, and board games. The time and the place cultivated closeness and growth as cold weather kept us in and connected while the lack of distracting personal devices harvested fruitful relationships. We had opportunity for real and lasting community.

So yes, some may say we didn't get the opportunity to learn how to dance (well, some of us poorly taught ourselves off of MTV) or join a school swim team (we always had Moon Lake!) or take YMCA sports clinics (the school was our teacher), but what we did have opportunity for was living in a place and time under unusual circumstances that made it possible to uniquely live in a way that very few people in America can say they did.

# The Many Men of Alaska:
# The Good and the Odd

My dad and my brother cutting wood for the winter.

Isn't there an old saying about Alaska men that "the odds are good but the goods are odd" when a woman comes inquiring about a husband? Well, that may be true in many parts of the state, but for some reason, Tok was a gold mine of good ones . . . and yes, perhaps a few odd. But in my circle of people, they were mostly good.

First and foremost of Alaskan men in my life was, of course, my dad. Memories of him stomping into the house during the dark of winter with his mustache frozen and frost around his hood still fill my senses if I let them. It was like winter came into the house with him. His outerwear was ice-cold, along with his cheeks and nose. Even with the hot wood stove burning, he gave off an air of winter. He gave off an air of Alaska.

I have memories of racing downstairs to the basement to watch some RATNET television. RATNET stood for Rural Alaska Television Network. What that meant was we had one channel on our television and it was a hodgepodge of stations. There was a nightly schedule of shows and news, and that was what we got . . . nothing more, nothing less. Unless the station tower went out. Then we had nothing. To get to the television, I had to run down the stairs, and at the bottom of the stairs, to my right, would often be my dad in his workshop. Maybe he'd be skinning martin and the aroma of martin lure hung in the air. Maybe he was patiently making bullets, with the smell of powder surrounding him. Maybe he was just fiddling around with whatever he kept down there. My dad in his workshop was a familiar sight, and the aromas that wafted from the open doorway were a familiar smell. My dad gave off the smell of the land, the smell of Alaska.

He faithfully hunted every fall to bring home meat for our family, and he fished for halibut and salmon. Rarely did the land not deliver, and we always had a freezer full of meat to keep us fed until spring. He was a good Alaskan man doing what he needed to do to keep his family fed and to keep his family warm. Many a day, he and my brother would be out at the woodpile, chopping away to collect our winter fuel. I as a child simply enjoyed the fierce heat of the wood stove, not realizing the strength, sweat, and labor that went into the warmth I so enjoyed.

My dad wasn't the only good man in the area, though. We had neighbors all the way up and down Borealis Avenue who measured right up to his goodness. We had teachers, business owners, friends, volunteers . . . and the list goes on. The men of Tok weren't interested just in their own welfare but in the welfare of others too, and that included us kids. Only later in life did some of us realize exactly what they did for us.

Our coaches worked full time and then took on coaching us kids in hockey, wrestling, basketball, and volleyball. They had families to provide for and care for, and then they had us. They and their families knew the importance of investing time in the future of Alaska. There were the men at church who said encouraging words, kind words, teasing words, and just plain old words. Some taught Sunday school, others spruced up the church building, and many simply showed up with their families to be a part of something bigger than themselves.

Wherever I was in Tok, they were there, some kind of good Alaskan man. They were doers in the Great Land, and they were givers too. Time was given, resources were spent, and most importantly, hearts were lent. So thank you to the good men of Alaska.

# The Wonderful Women of the North:
# The Tough and the Strong

Pat, Brenda, Patti, and my mom.

The women of Alaska are a beautiful thing. Growing up, I really had no clue what it meant to be a woman living in the cold and desolate interior. I was a little girl who only knew that it was dark and snowy all winter and light and dry all summer. I had my little group of friends and school to worry about, so living in Alaska was just as it was . . . a place to live wild and free and have cherished memories that I hold on to even today.

My mother told me a story of our first year living up there and how she had to make us powdered milk. I remembered that well. My brother and I choked it down, literally, the lumpy concoction (I can still smell that milk today) that came in the bright orange box with a smiling little girl on it. Lie! All a lie! Why was she smiling about drinking that milk? As a child, I felt cheated by the blatantly false advertising. What I didn't know was my mom's stern proclamation to my dad after a short time of ingesting that milk that if we could afford to live in Alaska, then we could afford to buy milk for the kids. After that, there was no more Milk Man powdered milk; it was replaced by a $4.99 gallon of milk several times a week. The year was 1982.

Looking back, I see that Alaskan-grown women were strong, and if the women were transplant Alaskans, then Alaska got right to work on making them strong. How? The isolation. The endless hours of dark and cold that kept people at home. The distance between loved ones left down in the States. The separation from husbands who worked in another city or on the North Slope or in the mines. The lack of shopping (food and clothing). The dependence on God and the land for food to make it through the winter. The lack of a doctor (although Tok was fortunate to have a wonderful physician assistant and nurse). Women were raising their children in a place where the nearest hospital was four or more hours away, sometimes even requiring travel by boat or by plane. In my opinion, a pregnant woman living in the bush of Alaska may very well be the bravest Alaskan of all.

Besides all of the difficulties that I can now reflect upon (and I know I didn't even list them all), what I remember are women who were present in my life: women like Patti, my junior high basketball coach, who sacrificed much as she coached and traveled with small children (pregnant one year and hauling the baby along on trips so she could coach us the next year); my teachers in Tok School and the office ladies who were constantly in my life, encouraging me, molding me, and caring for me; my piano teacher, who taught me after school; moms who opened their homes for dinners and sleepovers and group trips to Fairbanks for all of us girls to go shopping; the women in church who taught me about God and cooked food for our church potlucks and hugged me and welcomed me every single week.

And finally, my own mother, who set the example for me that I live today, that no matter where you go as a family, you go together, and that makes everything okay. I always knew my mother was a brave woman . . . a Midwestern girl who married a guy whose job and dream would lead him to Alaska, which meant she would go too. None of her family had ventured to live outside of the state of Wisconsin (except her dad, who pretty much went around the world during WWII), and there she was, practically going out of the country.

She may have moved to a place where it was dark and it was cold and milk was four times the cost, but she also moved to a place that gave her kids the most of their growing-up years. I frequently tell people that I had the most blessed and best childhood and I owe a good portion of that to her. She passed on her adventurous spirit to her children and taught us to live and love wherever we may be. She was a shining example of strength and support in a land faraway and beyond. She was an example of living and being present in the moment. She and many others were to me tough and strong wonderful women of the north.

# Daily Life

# Summertime Sunshine

My mom, me, and Cousin Tricia sunning in the Alaska summer sun . . . and probably swatting mosquitoes.

Contrary to popular belief, it does get warm in Alaska. Sometimes. Now, it may be for just a few weeks, but yes, the snow does melt and we teenagers (and adults, I'm sure) attempted to catch some rays with little to no effect on our skin color. I particularly sported a wonderful shade of Alaskan white and knew that my trips outside to Wisconsin and Iowa were my only hope of actually getting a real summer tan. I remember that in the month of May, there was still snow on the ground, because we girls in our high-heeled shoes would have to be extra careful as we headed out to prom. I think most of my prom shoes I had were water-stained (back then, we all had the dyed satin pumps to match our dresses) and had the heels all torn up from sinking into the gravel. Our shoes didn't stand a chance from the lingering winter, but who wanted to wear boots with their sequins?

June was the time when all of us kids started work, and by then it was warming up. Rain could be our companion at any time, however, and it wasn't exactly a welcome companion for me, who rode my bike to and from my place of employment.

By the time July rolled around, the rain had mostly ceased and it was actually plenty hot during the day. We could wear shorts and tank tops and even sandals, although I do remember biking home at night to beat my curfew all while freezing my toes off. My best friend and I would hunt for paper bags on the side of the road (which were plentiful because people would cast them aside from their liquor bottles) to put on our feet so we could stand the trip back. Maybe we should have just worn socks and sneakers instead . . . but it was summer. Sandal weather was but a short time in Alaska, so chilly evenings weren't going to sway us back into socks, no matter how cold our toes got.

Before we knew it, the calendar said August, and we knew our heat and even our sun would be fading away. By the time school started at the end of the month, the birch trees were wearing their full shade of yellow, the ground had gotten crunchy, my back-to-school shopping was done, and my wardrobe did not contain any hint of summer. Back to school in Alaska did not mean getting to wear shorts for the first few weeks. Nope. We were straight into full clothing, including winter jackets. It was usually cold by then.

Even though our summers were short, they were greatly welcomed and most certainly appreciated after the long, cold, dark, and sometimes very difficult winters. We relished the long, sun-filled days and made a point to soak it all up. We didn't take summer for granted, because we knew what was coming not far around the corner . . . a time of cold, but more importantly, for some, a time of darkness and isolation. We all were aware that cold with hours and hours of sunshine is much more bearable than cold shrouded in mostly darkness, but the latter was an Alaskan winter.

For us, summertime was a rejuvenating time, and rejuvenate we did. We planted gardens in our yards, and flowers around our homes. Summer was our time to store up for the winter, and not just in produce from our gardens, but also sunshine for our souls. But in reality, we couldn't *really* store up the sunshine. It was a nice thought and we tried. We may have canned tomatoes and freshly picked potatoes that we could store in our basement or cellar, but we couldn't put the sunlight in a jar. Just ask the people who sat under their sun lamps every day during the bitter-cold months of a dark winter just so they could make it to . . . you guessed it . . . summer.

# Normal Kids

Me in my room playing with a set of pink maracas.

I had a pen pal growing up who was from Michigan. I cannot remember if it was a boy or a girl, and I cannot even remember how long we corresponded. In fact, I'm not even sure now that this pen pal was from Michigan! But what I do remember were the questions that were asked of me by said pen pal. "Do you live in an igloo?" or "If you live in an igloo, how do you blow-dry your hair?" Those questions made me laugh because really, I was just a normal kid who blow-dried my hair just like everybody else. Now maybe it froze solid if it wasn't all the way dry on my way to the bus stop, but really, we were just normal kids in America.

Growing up, I pored over *Seventeen* and *Circus* magazines. My walls were plastered with posters of Bon Jovi, Poison, Def Leppard, and Warrant. I even had a see-through neon pink telephone mounted on my bedroom wall with an extra, extra long neon green cord so I could travel all over my room unhindered. My closet was full of clothes (particularly Guess, Esprit, and Bongo brands) and shoes, and I had a full-length mirror mounted on my wall so I could meticulously do my eighties hair and makeup every morning. There I would kneel as I scrunched the TRE-Semmé mousse into my spiral-permed hair and prepared to curl my bangs to perfection. I curled them, curled them again, and then curled them some more before I finally doused them with Aqua Net, Aussie, or Salon Selectives hair spray, until they stood stiff as a board to last through the hours of school, and maybe even basketball practice. I had one particular classmate in high school whose bangs were a whopping eight inches high! I could never compete. We measured one day with a ruler, and if she is reading this now, she knows I am talking about her.

My room was my sanctuary and my place of beauty and social readiness before my all-important appointment for school. It also housed all of my special things, my secret things. I had a huge junk box where I stored everything that meant anything, and my cassette stereo was always tuned to Armed Forces Radio (pretty much our only station) so I could memorize the latest tunes like Paula Abdul's "Straight Up" or Janet Jackson's "Rhythm Nation." That stereo lived on my bed at night as I pressed play on my mixed tape (side A and B) and set it to auto reverse so I could listen all night long to every single hair-band rock ballad I had recorded for my nightly sleeping ritual. A girl needed to have good dreams as she slept behind her black garbage bag-darkened windows.

I had a hamster, and I had parakeets. I had a fish that sat on my dresser. I had stuffed animals and dresser dolls and every prom champagne glass from school starting with the year 1989. I laughed in my room; I cried in my room. I had sleep-overs with friends (they showed up on their snow machines or four-wheelers, so I guess we weren't totally like the other kids in America), and I lost myself in a good book more times than I can count, reading into the wee morning hours. Yes, even in Alaska, in most respects we were just normal teens.

# When Ordinary was Exciting

Dad, Grandpa and Grandma Breeser, me, and Cid.

My mother-in-law stopped by one time for coffee after I had moved back to Washington, and our talk turned toward resourcefulness and the Great Depression. I shared with her how my grandma (my dad's mom) lived through the Depression and clung fast to the meager and frugal ways of life. She truly has never let go of them even to this day! I laughed as I retold a story about not finishing my dinner at her kitchen table in Iowa. That wasn't a problem for Grandma; she just scraped what I didn't eat onto my grandpa's plate and made him eat it. He grumbled but obliged her no-nonsense ways. Even her house tells a tale of living in a time of want. Every square inch of her home is covered in everything that was ever given to her. This woman who lived through a great time of need just couldn't find it in herself to waste a single thing, including wall space.

My mother-in-law then pointed out that living in Alaska probably instilled some resourcefulness in me too. How true that statement was! When you live in a small town four hours away from the nearest city, you learn how to plan, make do, or simply do without. This is where duct tape came in quite handy. Sometimes, we had to be quite imaginative in our small town when resources weren't available.

Living in Tok, you didn't just "run out" and pick up a new shirt for work or a pair of sneakers for gym class. Sometimes you couldn't even get milk at the store. I knew that during the weekend we went school shopping in Fairbanks, I'd better get everything I wanted or needed, because the next time I'd get a new shirt or pair of jeans or the latest cassette tape would be under the Christmas tree four months later. I remember calling my mom many years later after I moved into the University of Idaho dorms, totally enthralled with the fact that I could walk to a mall and buy a shirt any time I wanted to. What a concept!

Clothing wasn't the only thing we needed, though. Before the snow flew, my parents made a trip to Anchorage, where they brought home a fully loaded vehicle from Costco. It was like Christmastime when they pulled up with the back packed tight to the roof with Top Ramen, juice boxes, granola bars, pasta, fruit snacks, toilet paper, and everything else to make it through the hard winter months. We gladly helped them haul in the goods and then excitedly put it all away down on our food shelves in the basement. How could anyone be so excited about supplies? Just ask a kid who grew up in a remote area, and they will tell you why. Because we had such limited access to groceries and goods, we learned to be content with what we had, and that made some things that were very ordinary and easily accessible to people "outside" very, very special to us.

There was also the unpopular option of ordering clothing and supplies from a catalog, but we didn't do that very often since shipping seemed to cost more than the item desired and the time of arrival was most certainly not guaranteed. Just ask my mom, who ordered a Wheel of Fortune board game that arrived weeks after Christmas. That didn't stop us from poring over the Sears Christmas catalog that came in the mail, though. My brother and I searched every page of that book until its edges were tattered and earmarked and we'd underlined or circled every possible thing we wanted. One time I even called and placed a big order through JC Penney (hey, I had cash on my dresser), only to find out I needed a credit card to finish my purchase. I sheepishly hung up the phone, imagining that the woman on the other end was more than annoyed with me. There were just a whole lot of things we wanted that we just couldn't get because of where we lived. That was why grocery store items became exciting purchases and overnight trips into "town" were, in our lives, quite normal. Yes, we were resourceful, planned ahead, and made do in Alaska, and it wasn't because of circumstances like the Great Depression but rather because of our choice . . . our choice to live in Alaska.

# Hunting and Living Off the Land

Dad packing moose antlers.

Many memories of my childhood are entwined with my dad and his love for hunting, fishing, and trapping. Every year, he went out to bring back either caribou or moose for our family to make it through the winter. He would be gone for days and days, and after each hunt, I marveled at his stories, whether they were about hauling a moose out of a lake to help a fellow hunter (involving inflatable tubes and a very wet guy) or packing hundreds of pounds of meat out on foot. The tales were fascinating, and the meat was fresh and plentiful. Many times, we processed it ourselves (it isn't easy hand-grinding burger, just so you know), and my job was always to tape what one of the adults wrapped up in white paper and then write the date and what part of the animal it was and then run it out to the freezer in our heated garage. Then after all was said and done, my dad would make his own moose or caribou jerky that my brother and I learned real quick we could barter to get anything we wanted during school lunchtime. I can still remember the smell of caribou steak wafting through the house as my mom fried it up for dinner.

Hunting trips would take my dad and sometimes my brother away for a week at a time. They would fly into Molly Creek and camp at the airstrip, which was basically a clear spot of acreage for the planes to land on. The pilots would drop off my dad and brother and then leave. There were usually a few sets of hunters looking for caribou at the same time. Each day, my dad and brother would access the bluffs or watch for caribou to come across the saddles in the mountains. There they would sit and wait until one came into their sights. After the animal was shot and quartered, they would haul the meat back to camp on foot, usually a few miles away, and strap the meat and antlers on the outside of the airplane or wherever it would fit, and then they would fly back home.

My dad also went halibut fishing out of Homer and brought home about one hundred pounds of meat, which I can honestly say I was quite sick of by the end of the winter. He would also dip net for salmon in Chitna. The game and fish were abundant in Alaska. It was clear to see how abundant, when we were fishing on the Copper River and saw a dog eating as well as his owner. It wasn't uncommon to see people feeding their dogs salmon. People down in the States would pay $20.00 a pound for that!

Dad, dip netting on the Copper River.

Hunting, fishing, and trapping were part of our survival. Living off the land wasn't something we did for sport, it was something we did for necessity. Like many families in Tok, we knew that winter was coming and we needed to be ready. Ready to live. Ready to endure. Ready to survive.

# Tok:
# A Little Pocket of
# Something Wonderful

# Bucky the Moose:
# Forever in Our Hearts

Grandpa Breeser on Bucky the Moose.

**M**ost cities have some sort of fixture that makes them distinct. For example, San Francisco has the Golden Gate Bridge and Seattle has the Space Needle. There is the giant arch in St. Louis, and New York City has the Statue of Liberty. Well, Tok, not to be outdone by the great cities of this nation, was no exception. We had Bucky the Moose in all of his glory.

I don't even know when Bucky first arrived in Tok, but I can tell you that in the early eighties, he was not only a star but was already quite mangy and worn out. Bucky was a giant stuffed moose that sat out in front of the Golden Bear Motel. He had a saddle and a convenient wood stump for people to climb on to hoist themselves onto his back. Sure, thousands of tourists sat on Bucky's back over the years and took their pictures, but us local kids never tired of the novelty moose. It was always fun to swing up onto his back and slurp down the Slush Puppies we had bought at the local store, "riding" one, two, and three friends deep.

Bucky was a tall, tall moose. It wasn't easy to scramble up onto him, but even my grandparents from Iowa managed to mount the moose for a picture to take home to their neighbors who wouldn't believe it unless they saw it with their own eyes. Sometime after I had graduated from high school, I heard through the local grapevine that Bucky had become some sort of a legend. He simply up and disappeared (which means he got so mangy that somebody took him and dropped him in the dump). Who then took him out of the dump remains a mystery (kind of), but if there is one thing I know for certain, it is that *someone* had a broad sense of Alaskan humor. This person or people set poor Bucky up on the side of the road for hunters to be fooled.

According to local folklore, shots did abound, and Bucky took his fair share of hits. He was far enough away from the highway so he looked like a living moose but close enough to tempt any trigger-happy hungry Alaskan to pull over and grab the rifle off the gun rack to take aim. Well, he stayed out there long enough to become a legend. I don't know when Bucky was removed and where his final resting place was (probably back at the dump), but does it really matter? Bucky is right here in my heart and in the hearts of people all over. He's especially in the hearts not only of those who sat on his back on warm summer days, but also of the folks who stopped their vehicles, took aim, and shot at that mangy mammoth of a moose.

# Mukluk Land: One Unique Destination

Me and Cid at Mukluk Land.

My husband started chatting with his dad's neighbor one weekend and discovered that he had spent some time living in Alaska. Finding common ground, my husband told him that I had grown up in Alaska and, upon the neighbor inquiring where, informed him that I had lived in Tok. "Tok? There is nothing in Tok!" the man exclaimed.

My husband may have laughed, because he has yet to visit my much-loved town, but I heartily disagree. Besides Bucky the Moose (God rest his soul) and many, many, exciting qualities, Tok has Mukluk Land. I started working at Mukluk Land when I was in the sixth grade and continued on for several years after. During the summer, I'd hop on my bike and pedal several miles for my one o'clock start time (also the time the park opened). It was exciting to take my place behind the counter at the skee ball shack as Gary, the owner's son, marched out to undo the yellow plastic chain that looped across the sawdust-trailed entryway into the park. Sometimes kids were lined up, and sometimes not, but no matter what, we were ready.

Mukluk Land had miniature "bush" golf, and a bouncy house shaped like an igloo. You could even take a ride on a dog sled pulled by a four-wheeler. You could walk the trail to see the Tent in Tok (an erected army tent the Bernhardt family spent a winter in), gaze upon the world's largest mosquito, and study a lot of really great museum pieces (old snow machines and the like). The snack shack at the back of the park always had fresh popcorn and cotton candy, and you could sit in the little back room and watch a video of the northern lights while you enjoyed your treat. Afterward, you could visit the small gift shop to purchase a reminder of Alaska, as if your visit wasn't enough! You could even pan for gold at the park (it was guaranteed)! Then before you left (or even upon arrival), Beth or George, the wonderful owners, would be sure to have you put a stick pin in the world map to show where you had visited from. Even back then, the map had

My brother, Cid, and Uncle Mike "holding" up the giant mukluk at Mukluk Land.

gotten impressively full. So many people from all over the world leaving their mark for others to see. Oh, and don't forget the world's largest mukluk gracing the entrance to the park.

I'm pretty sure all or most of this is still available in Tok, with probably even more added, so, neighbor of my father-in-law who used to live in Alaska, there absolutely is something in Tok!

# The Mukluk News

♥ ♥ ♥ ♥ ♥ ♥ ♥ ♥ ♥ ♥♥

## Memorial Service Held
### for Steve Breeser

Memorial services were held at Faith Chapel in Tok on Sunday, April 7 at 6 p.m., for Steve Breeser, 46, who passed away April 4 of complications of leukemia at the Dartmouth-Hitchcock Medical Center in Lebanon, New Hampshire.

The Reverend Paul Milanowski officiated assisted by the Reverend Terry Pruett. Jan Persson and Paul Milanowski sang "It Is Well with My Soul" accompanied by Cam Bohman on the piano. The congregation sang, "The Lord Is My Shepherd" and "I Know Who Holds Tomorrow." Melinda Rallo read the obituary and Randy Rallo video taped the service. Helen Windus-Olson, Melinda Rallo, and Cam Bohman also shared special memories. The service concluded with Solveig and Gustaf Olson playing "Taps" on their trumpets.

ALCA

"We Bu

Satu

P

Case Lots

Miner

Trad

The memorial service article that was published in the *Mukluk News* for my dad.

Every town needs a paper, and Tok was no exception. The Mukluk News was started in 1976 by George and Beth Jacobs (also the owners of Mukluk Land). The idea was born at a church potluck. A few of the folks were sitting around discussing what was the current newspaper in Tok, and someone mentioned that the paper did not represent all sides on the election issues.

An English teacher at the time told George Jacobs that if George would print the paper, Beth and she, the teacher, would publish it. That night, the Mukluk News was born. The first papers were typed on an electric typewriter, and the Jacobses traveled to Anchorage to purchase a mimeograph machine to print it. Any type of printing press equipment they purchased for Tok came by way of their pickup truck. To this day, the paper has always been written and printed with Tok, Dot Lake, Tanacross, Mentasta, Northway, Tetlin, Chicken, Border, and Eagle in mind.

I remember as a kid being eager for each and every printing. You could pick up a copy around town, and at first, the papers were only available at the local businesses that advertised with the *Mukluk News*. George and Beth would drop them off, and the businesses would sell them. Eventually, George and Beth built a subscription list, but even today, they still take papers to their local advertisers. That's how I remember getting our news—at the local grocery store, unless they had run out, and then we'd have to hop around town to the other businesses to see if we could find one. The paper was a very important part of our community connection.

The *Mukluk News* was and is what a small-town paper should be. How many times did I see a write-up about our sporting events or school concerts? It was a go-to source for what was happening around town. Churches, schools, and organizations announced their activities, and new businesses received a special highlight. I will never forget when a bakery opened in Tok. A bakery, of all things! Fresh donuts and bread daily. Who would have thought?

Death, wedding, and birth announcements were also a significant part of our local paper. After my dad passed away, I wrote his obituary for the *Mukluk News*, and even though I had been gone for four years, it was important for me to do. Here is an excerpt from the obituary:

> *Oh how Steve loved the wilds. Working as a U.S. Fish and Wildlife Manager he collared moose, tagged wolves and banded ducks, always chasing down some animal. He worked along the "Upper Miss" and then on into the best deer hunting country in the nation, Medicine Lake, Montana. He romped through low-bush cranberry and spruce topped mountains of Alaska. Finally, he opened a refuge on Lake Umbagog, for the only two nesting bald eagles in New England.*

Growing up, we would pore over the trooper and court reports, and search for the funny jokes and comics hidden through the pages. It was particularly meaningful to read the paper when we were in an article or if we had been involved in the production of the actual paper. What a privilege when George and Beth would call up some of us local kids to come over and help collate and staple the *Mukluk News*. My brother and I would either get dropped off by our parents or madly pedal down the one-mile dirt road from our house to theirs, where we'd take a left into their driveway marked by large colorful pencils (made out of trees) for an evening of working on the paper.

Between the talking and working, we produced an enormous (in our eyes) stack of news to deliver to businesses and mail to subscribers, over 200 of them, just like they do today. Some people had the luxury of the paper being mailed to them in Tok, but most of the subscriptions were mailed to different places in the state, and quite a few out of state and even some to Canada. Back then, you could pick up the *Mukluk* for $0.35. Today it's a whopping $0.50. I think maybe it's about time I got on that mailing list.

# The Tok Choral Society

Me, Mary and Jan singing music from *Oliver Twist*.

Tok may have had only a K–12 school for the kids, but the University of Alaska Fairbanks had a branch in Tok that allowed the community and even some of us kids to take some classes. I joined the Tok Choral Society and fondly recall the joy of learning how to be in a show choir. We performed in the Tok School gym dressed up in poodle skirts like we were from the fifties, and my love for singing, acting, and performing was lit on fire. The choir was a mix of young and old, but we all had a similar passion, and that passion was music.

Another time, we performed the music from *Oliver Twist* at the K–8 school in Tanacross. I had a solo singing "Ripe Strawberries Ripe" with my pink bonnet and brown wicker basket in the marketplace with Oliver. My last performance with the Tok Choral Society took place at my church, Faith Chapel. We formed a ragtime band, sang "The Purple People Eater" and donned some pretty festive ragtime hats. We didn't have theater at Tok School (although we did have an annual Christmas play at our church), so with the Tok Choral Society, some of us kids got to stretch our wings and fly a little farther than maybe we thought we ever could. The choir was pure fun and a most welcome activity in our community, bringing all different personalities together for a little bit of entertainment that the whole town and surrounding areas could enjoy.

Tok Choral Society performing. I am part of the ragtime band.

# The Tok Race of Champions

A musher and his team during the Tok Race of Champions.

T he Tok Race of Champions has been going for sixty years strong. As a kid, I tagged along with my parents to the races, leaning against the fence, watching the mushers take off. It was just another day in Tok for me, an event my parents took me to. Little did I know back then what an important and special race this was. Taking place during the month of March, the Tok Race of Champions is one of the longest-held dog mushing races in Alaska. There is also the Junior Race of Champions, encouraging kids in the competitive sport of sprint mushing. With dog mushing such a rich part of Alaskan history, Tok is right in the heart of keeping such an important part of native culture alive and well.

A musher taking off. The Dog Musher's Building is in the back-
ground. We had our Easter pancake breakfast in that building
every year. See the American and Canadian flags?

# The Tok Trot

Paul Kelley giving me my Tok Trot button.

Most people who live or have lived in Tok have participated in the Tok Trot at one time or another, or at least thought of participating. Paul Kelley started the race in 1981, one year before we moved there. This ten-kilometer race that you can even walk if you'd like has been a staple of the community for over thirty years. I walked the trot as a kid, and one time I was so slow that they had to come pick me up because the race was more than over. I still got my Tok Trot button, though, and had my fill of food at the Kelleys' after race potluck (which still happens today). People who have moved away since then and loved living in Tok do the Tok Trot wherever they might be to keep that connection to Tok alive, to feel a part of the community that they once were a part of. The race has been run all over the world. One of the most memorable races was not run in Tok but rather in Baghdad in the green zone.

The race was and still is run in April because earlier than that it's too cold and later than that, people are too busy with fishing, hunting, traveling, and working. The race starts at the visitor's center in Tok and goes down the highway 3.1 miles and then comes back. People have skied, Rollerbladed, roller-skated, and wheeled (in a wheelchair) the Tok Trot. The runners come from all over, even as far as Whitehorse, Canada, but most of the walkers, like me, were local Tok people doing our local Tok thing and collecting our wonderful Tok Trot buttons.

# The Tok River Fire

Smoke from the fire burning not too far in the distance.

I wasn't there for the infamous Tok River Fire. I was thousands of miles away in Wisconsin for my "outside" trip to visit family that summer. Although I missed the most intense days, I remember holding my breath in July of 1990, watching Tok on the national news as my parents instructed my brother on what to take from the house as the whole town was evacuated to the Tanacross airport, a native village about twelve miles west of Tok.

If I remember correctly, a lightning strike started the fire that eventually burned out of control, jumping rivers and charging straight toward Tok, forcing the emergency evacuation. My brother got the call to get out pretty early in the day. That meant it was time to move, so he told his boss at the Westmark that he had to go load up and load out.

My brother recalls vehicles lined up on the runway just waiting for news and for what to do next. He took all the guns, documents, photo albums, and wall art in case the fire reached our home. To top it off, he had our dog, Annie, and his black cat, Bebop, loose in the truck cab, with Bebop jumping out the window every chance she got. My brother clearly remembers Bob McCarthy, our elderly school janitor, stationed on the highway and directing traffic. Bob would let people out but would not let people in.

During the days before the height of the Tok fire, the town got overwhelmed by firefighters coming to help. The firefighters ended up at the BLM pump station (our home during our first three years in Tok), where they lived in a gigantic tent city. The local restaurants helped out with feeding them, and Tokites rented out extra vehicles for the fire service to use. The firefighters built huge firebreak lines all around the town to try to stop the fire from crossing over and destroying everything in its path.

Smoke and flames looming over Tok.

A classmate of my brother later told him wild stories of supplying fuel to the fire-fighters. His parents owned a fuel station in Tok, and he would help drive the fuel trucks down, with flames licking at them on each side of the road. It was an odd and surreal time, with the smoke and ash thickly coating everything in sight. Every-thing smelled everywhere. Nothing was immune from the smoke. People's eyes were irritated, and breathing was difficult as the smoke settled in a thick, deep covering like a dense early morning fog. The town was a reddish-orange, and the smoke would be so thick at points that one couldn't see the Tok Junction from the Westmark hotel, which was literally right on the corner of the junction. If someone pulled up to get on the road from a side street, they couldn't see if a car was coming. People in Tok during that time had to drive with their lights on 24/7, and for summer in Alaska, that was simply unheard of.

What looked like a surefire tragedy soon became legend as a "miracle wind" saved my tiny town. I get emotional writing about it even now, over twenty-five years later. As residents fled and the flames leapt higher and faster, bound and determined to eat up our town, a few of the residents gathered by the junction and grabbed hands and prayed. Then, to the wonder of all, the flag that had been blowing strong and steady toward town shifted and blew the other way. The fire was turned and eventually burned out without consuming our homes and businesses or our people. Our little town was safe because on that very hot day in July where all seemed lost, God showed up just in time.

# Leaving Alaska

# Our Future

Me on my eighth birthday, surrounded by neighbors
from the BLM pump station.

Over thirty years ago, I sat at our dining room table in Tok and blew out my birthday candles. At the tender age of eight, I had no idea what the future would hold. I just knew that neighbors came to celebrate with me and that my mom baked me a cake and soon it would be time to open my presents. I was simply growing up. I spent my days out at the BLM pump station on my bike playing cops and robbers, and my evenings attempting to win at various outdoor games. I knew my summertime birthday was good. There was endless daylight to do what I needed to do, which was simply to play.

When I was a child, I didn't think about what was to come, what challenges and joys I would face on life's journey. I concerned myself with what cereal there was for breakfast and if my neighbor friend Joe could come over to play. I ran into the woods, my constant playground, not even considering that I could come face to face with a moose or a bear. It was a grand adventure, and my little heart knew it. I scrambled up the giant hill behind our old apartments to munch on raspberries with no regard for time. I was free, my mind was uncluttered, and worry was no companion of mine.

Sometimes I look back at momentous times in my life like a birthday or high school graduation or my wedding day and think about what I did not know then that I do know now. In 1983, on that birthday so long ago, I didn't know that during my senior year, I would move out of Alaska to the distant land of New Hampshire. If you would've told me I would be gone from Alaska, I would have looked at you like you had just told me that I was going to live on the moon. Years later, it happened, and before I knew it, I was standing on a different stage in a different state, completing my high school education and peering wide-eyed into my future as an adult.

When I graduated from high school, my adopted daughter had already been born and was living down in Texas. Little did I know as I walked across that stage to get my diploma that I was already a mom. I just wouldn't meet her for another fifteen years. On that same graduation day, with my parents smiling up at me, I had no clue that fewer than three years later, I would lose my dad to cancer. I was still in my carefree world (although now it had gotten a little cluttered with going off to college and mooning over boys). Then I was off to the University of Idaho (the

Me and Jenny Keazer graduating from Colebrook Academy, Colebrook, NH.

school I was going to go to after I graduated from Tok), and it wasn't long before I was engaged to be married. In 1996 when I said my "I dos," I didn't know that our oldest adopted son had just been born two weeks prior. He teases us now that we had to get married because of him . . . even though it would be twelve years before we even knew he existed.

Could I even imagine what life had in store for me? On my wedding day, we had two kids we didn't even know about yet, and they weren't even in the state that we lived in! Ten years later, we moved to Texas, and that day in August when we drove into Houston, our youngest son was born (the brother of our teenagers). We literally arrived and settled in a city a few miles from the hospital where he was at. He was not even a thought in our minds but was most certainly a thought in God's. It was seventeen months later when he would cross over the threshold of our home and become the doorway for his two older brothers and an older sister to become a part of our family. When we rolled into the great state of Texas (although not nearly as great as Alaska), we didn't realize so much more was happening than graduate school, but isn't that how life tends to be?

As a child or even a teenager, I never in a million years would have dreamed that I would move out of Alaska, lose my dad at such a young age, eventually live in Texas, adopt six kids out of foster care, and end up settling down in Spokane, Washington, to raise my family. If someone would have sent me a birthday card thirty years ago spelling out my future, I would have thrown those crazy ideas to the side for my mother to read and then torn into my presents. But here I am, more than thirty years after I blew out those candles in Tok, with a mind not as carefree and uncluttered but, I think, even more full of wonder. As for my heart? Well, it most certainly remains a heart full of faith and love, and it's just as ready for more grand adventures.

# Good-bye

The double rainbow sending us off.

I t came as a surprise to me when my parents announced we were moving out of Alaska and taking our journey to New Hampshire. As a kid, I never even thought about living anywhere else. My life in Tok was all I had known except for fleeting memories of Montana. Plus, I was heading into my senior year. What was this talk about moving? My dad, whose dream was to live in Alaska, apparently also had a dream to start a wildlife refuge. Unbeknownst to me, my dad had been tracking a potential job on the east coast for two years, and it had finally come to fruition. Our time in Alaska was coming to an end.

I did in some respects go kicking and screaming, but I was also my father's daughter, and the spirit of adventure lay in my heart just as it lay in his. On moving day, we pulled out and down Main Street Tok, and as we departed the place that I loved, I leaned my forehead against the window of the club cab of our burgundy truck and watched my best friend wave from a parking lot as we drove out of sight. She was the last friend I saw that day as I balanced my fish on my lap in his bowl (yes,

I sat like that the *whole* way to New Hampshire) and resigned myself to capturing my final memories of Alaska that way.

Earlier, we had stopped just outside of town at an airstrip close to our house right after a rainstorm and my mom had captured a picture of a double rainbow. A double rainbow appeared when we began our journey out of the wilds of Alaska. I believe it was God's blessing on our time spent in Tok and that it was a message that it was okay to go even though it was tearing my heart out. We had done what we were supposed to do, and it was time to move on.

It would be much later on, after I'd grown up just a little bit more, when I would realize that watching my town disappear out of sight from the back of our burgundy truck would yes, be my final memories of living in Alaska, but not of Alaska itself. The spirit of Alaska lives on in me and in those who have called it home. I've visited twice since I left, making new memories, and have kept in touch with many of the people who make Alaska, well, Alaska. I've connected with Alaskans all over this country, and every time we speak, we find that a kindred spirit exists between us. So even though it has been years since I said my good-byes, I can see now that it was more of a "see you later." If you have ever lived in Alaska, you never really say good-bye.

# Going Home

My mom and me at the Women's Alcan Retreat in 2006.

When I first moved out of Alaska, it was to northern New Hampshire, a beautiful state with plenty of snow and below-zero temperatures. In some respects, it helped me feel like I had not totally abandoned my extreme northern roots. After my senior year in New Hampshire, I went to college in northern Idaho, where I had planned to go after graduating from Tok. Alaska and Idaho had a sister-school program so you could attend school in either place for in-state tuition.

Eventually, I settled in eastern Washington with my husband. I did feel more removed from Alaska by now with our milder winters, but I still had snow at times, and beautiful land all around me. I had visited Alaska only once (in 1994, for Elizabeth, my best friend's high school graduation) since I had moved "outside," but it would be twelve long years after that visit before I would return to my hometown of Tok.

That particular year (2006), I had felt a yearning to visit Alaska. My husband and I were in the process of picking a graduate school for him to attend, and I knew wherever we ended up going would be somewhere quite far away from the Pacific Northwest. As I sat and pondered a visit, not knowing how it could ever happen with two small children at home and a rather large cross-country move on the horizon, I did the only thing that seemed right to do. I prayed. It wasn't too much later when I received an out-of-the-blue phone call from my mom in Wisconsin about an opportunity to travel back to Alaska to help with the annual Alcan Women's Retreat in Tok. She had been asked to speak. I knew immediately that I was to go. Hadn't my heart already told me I would? Was I finally getting to return to Main Street Alaska, as Tok is fondly known? I offered to help with the music for the retreat, and plans were on the way.

The Alcan Women's Retreat was a very special time for some of the ladies in Tok and the surrounding areas. I distinctly remember those yearly retreats while I was growing up as women trekked in from the bush to Tok's little Faith Chapel to gather with other women who had made it through the winter for a time of connecting and sharing.

As travel arrangements fell into place, I grew more and more excited to return to the land I had left so long ago. It was a trip I would never forget. When the day finally arrived to head north to Alaska, it began to sink in that I was going home. When I boarded the plane in Seattle, I was full of nervous excitement. You see, Alaska never, ever gets out of your blood, and it never leaves your heart. I hadn't been back for twelve years, and the anticipation was palpable.

I sat down next to a North Sloper, which made me smile. I didn't even have to ask, I just knew. He had an air about him that spoke of the very far north. You could feel it. He was heading back to work for his three-week stint, content in his seat to watch the scenery pass by. We chatted here and there about life way up north as my eyes were riveted by the mountains outside my plane window. About an hour into the trip, I leaned over him to drink in the mountains . . . the hundreds of mountains that went so deep and wide . . . and he smiled at me. The vastness, the depth, and the beauty were breathtakingly familiar. Memories rushed back, and my childhood rested before my eyes as I took in the glorious view. I shared my story of growing up in Tok and how it had been so long since I had gone home.

As we began our descent into Anchorage, I got uncharacteristically quiet and unashamedly misty-eyed as I gazed out the plastic plane window. I couldn't help it;

tears sprang to my eyes and a lump formed in my throat. That old North Sloper with his kind twinkling eyes and understanding smile leaned over and ever so quietly and gently said, "Welcome home." He was right. Yes indeed, yes indeed, I was home.

Here's to the genuine joy of coming home . . . . Here's to *Growing up Alaska*.

# About the Author:
# Niki Breeser Tschirgi

Niki Breeser Tschirgi is a stay-at-home mom who resides in Spokane, Washington, with her husband and six adopted kids (five still at home, ages eight through eighteen, all boys). She discovered her love for writing in the seventh grade and studied Creative Writing at the University of Idaho. Niki wrote for *Blindigo Online Magazine* while living in Houston, Texas, and over the years, has published several blogs such as "The Stars Are Bright—How a Northern Girl Became a Southern Woman and Everything Inbetween" and "Rock a Child's World," which raised awareness for adoption in Texas. Her most current blogs can be read at www.spokandyland.com and www.growingupalaska.net. To connect with Niki and learn more about life in Alaska, follow her on Facebook: www.facebook.com/growingupalaska or Twitter: @nikitschirgi.

CPSIA information can be obtained at www.ICGtesting.com
Printed in the USA
BVOW08s0448090615

403750BV00004B/10/P